A Political Memoir of the Anglo-French

Condominium of the New Hebrides

A Political Memoir of the Anglo-French Condominium of the New Hebrides

Keith Woodward

Published by ANU Press
The Australian National University
Canberra ACT 0200, Australia
Email: anupress@anu.edu.au
This title is also available online at http://press.anu.edu.au

National Library of Australia Cataloguing-in-Publication entry

Author: Woodward, Keith, author.

Title: A political memoir of the Anglo-French condominium of the New Hebrides / Keith Woodward.

ISBN: 9781925021981 (paperback) 9781925022209 (ebook)

Subjects: Woodward, Keith.
Decolonization--Vanuatu.
Vanuatu--Politics and government.
Great Britain--Colonies--Oceania.
France--Colonies--Oceania.

Dewey Number: 995.95

All rights reserved. No part of this publication may be reproduced, stored in a retrieval system or transmitted in any form or by any means, electronic, mechanical, photocopying or otherwise, without the prior permission of the publisher.

Cover design and layout by ANU Press

This edition © 2014 ANU Press

Contents

List of Illustrations. vii

List of Acronyms. ix

Dedication xi

Biography of Keith Woodward. xiii

Preface xv
    Margaret Jolly

Author's Acknowledgements xvii

A Political Memoir of the Anglo-French Condominium of the
    New Hebrides 1

References 91

List of Illustrations

Figures

1	Keith Woodward, portrait. Photographer Fleur Woodward, July 2014.	xiii
2	British Paddock with Administration offices. Photographer Michael Allen, November 1958.	2
3	War Memorial, Port Vila, Iririki Island in background. Photographer Michael Allen, November 1958.	3
4	Roman Catholic cathedral, Port Vila. Photographer Michael Allen, November 1958.	4
5	French Hospital lower-right side, Port Vila. Photographer Michael Allen, November 1958.	4
6	The Joint Court, Port Vila 1973—formerly the residence of the President of the Court. Photographer Brian Bresnihan.	5
7	Burns Philp's pier and Iririki Island on right. Photographer Michael Allen, November 1958.	8
8	Keith Woodward and unidentified friend at one of Port Vila's nearby beaches. Photographer Michael Allen, November 1958.	9
9	The *Polynésie*, from the Rossi Hotel, Port Vila waterfront. Photographer Michael Allen, November 1958.	11
10	Eratoka Island, also known as Hat Island, Ghost Island or Devil's Island taken from aboard the *Don Quixote*. Photographer Michael Allen, November 1958.	81
11	Jean Guiart writing up his diary in Maroo village, Emau Island. Photographer Michael Allen, November 1958.	81
12	Keith Woodward and John Champion, the British Resident Commissioner at Bauerfield Airport, Port Vila, on the day of Keith's departure from the New Hebrides, 1 March, 1978. Photographer unknown, supplied by Brian Bresnihan.	86
13	From left: Keith Woodward, Dick Baker and Brian Bresnihan (all colleagues in the British Administration), framed by unidentified New Hebrideans, including an airline official in the bottom right hand corner. Keith was on the point of checking in for his flight on the day of his departure from the New Hebrides. Bauerfield Airport, 1 March, 1978. Photographer unknown, supplied by Brian Bresnihan.	86

14 Keith enjoying himself at a lunch party in Port Vila in March 1980, when he paid a return visit to the New Hebrides. He is talking to Olla Reeve, the woman who painted the watercolour of The British Office (Figure 15). Photographer Brian Bresnihan. 88

15 British Administration Building, watercolour, Olla Reeve, in the collection of Brian Bresnihan. Photographer Brian Bresnihan. 89

Table

1 The retention by the NP of its two Santo Rural seats, despite the fact that it did not have a majority in the electorate, was mainly due to the splitting of the anti-NP vote by the participation in the contest of Tabwemassana and Fren Melanesian party candidates. 62

List of Acronyms

AdCo	Advisory Council
BP	Burns Philp
BR	British Residency
BRC	British Resident Commissioner
CD1	Central District No.1 (Epi, Shepherd Group and Efate Island.)
CD2	Central District No. 2 (Malekula, Ambrym, Pentecost and Paama)
CFNH	Comptoirs Français des Nouvelles-Hébrides
DCA	Department of Civil Aviation (Australian)
DOM/TOM	The French Ministry dealing with New Hebrides affairs
EDC	Electoral Disputes Committee
FM	Fren Melanesian
FR	French Residency
FRC	French Resident Commissioner
HQ	Headquarters
LegCo	Legislative Council
JR	Joint Regulation
MANH	Mouvement pour L'Autonomie des Nouvelles-Hébrides
MSG	Melanesian Spearhead Group – a governmental organisation consisting of the four Melanesian states of Fiji, Papua New Guinea, Solomon Islands, Vanuatu and the Kanak and Socialist National Liberation Front of New Caledonia.
MTN	MANH/Tabwemasana/Nagriamel Alliance
ND	Northern District (Santo, Ambae, Maevo, Banks and Torres)
NGF	Nagriamel Federation
NP	National Party
NP/VP	National Party/Vanuaku Party
PPG	People's Provisional Government
RA	Representative Assembly
SD	Southern District (Aneityum, Aniwa, Erromango, Futuna and Tanna)
SDAs	Seventh Day Adventists
SFNH	Société Française des Nouvelles-Hébrides
SPADES	South Pacific Action for Development Strategy
UCHN	Union des Communautés des Nouvelles-Hébrides
UNELCO	Union Electrique Coloniale des Nouvelles-Hébrides
UPNH	Union des Populations des Nouvelles-Hébrides
VP	Vanuaku Party/Vanu'aku Pati (Bislama)

To my wife Elizabeth
who painstakingly corrected
my original typescript

Biography of Keith Woodward

Figure 1. Keith Woodward, portrait.

Source: Photograph by Fleur Woodward, July 2014.

Keith Woodward was born in Ismailia, Egypt in 1930. He was educated at Probus School, Plymouth College and Keble College, Oxford, graduating in Modern History in 1951. In 1953 he joined the British National Service in the New Hebrides as office assistant, was promoted to be Assistant Secretary in 1957, and Administrative Officer, Class A in 1970. Woodward dealt with a wide variety of administrative matters during his twenty-five years at the British Residency, including Condominium Personnel, Agriculture, District Affairs, Land, Education, Health and Constitutional Development, holding the post of Secretary for Political Affairs from 1968, until his retirement (because of failing eyesight) in 1978. He had a major part in setting up the Port Vila Cultural Centre (1961–62), and was Hon. Secretary to the Board of Management for sixteen years. He was also much involved with the introduction of Scouting (under the aegis of the British Commonwealth Scouting Movement), serving from 1956 as secretary to the Scout Council and later as Chairman. Woodward was awarded the MBE in 1964, the OBE in 1976 and the Vanuatu Independence Medal in 1980. Keith lives in retirement in Bath, UK.

Preface

This is a fascinating memoir written by Keith Woodward many years after he left the then New Hebrides where he worked for almost twenty-five years in the British Administration. Although he is modest about his own contributions in these years, Keith played a significant role in the moves towards self-government, an innovative, electoral system and ultimately, in 1980, independence when the country became Vanuatu. This work not only led to his award of an OBE but a Vanuatu Independence Medal. It will be an invaluable history not just for those ni-Vanuatu who lived through those momentous and turbulent years leading up to independence but for those of subsequent generations. It will also be a great resource for scholars of the decolonisation process and political history of Vanuatu and the Pacific more broadly. In addition, it highlights the complexity of the relations between British and French colonialisms in the archipelago and the region.

I would like to thank both Brian Bresnihan and Michael Allen for their excellent photos from the period and Keith's daughter Fleur for the recent photograph of her father. I am also grateful to Brian for permission to reproduce his photograph of the painting of the British Administration buildings by Olla Reeve which is in his collection. I thank Mitiana Arbon for his excellent cover design using two historical photographs provided by Brian and Michael respectively.

Thanks also to Stewart Firth the Chair of the Pacific Editorial Board of ANU Press and its members for their enthusiasm about this book and the excellent insights and positive suggestions which came from two anonymous readers, whom we now know were Howard Van Trease and Gregory Rawlings. Finally, I must thank my colleague Carolyn Brewer who has as always done an excellent job of copyediting of the manuscript and conversion to ANU Press style with grace and speed and ANU Press staff for their prompt and professional shepherding of this book to publication.

Margaret Jolly
23 July 2014

Author's Acknowledgements

I am grateful to The Australian National University for publishing this memoir, and so conferring on it a totally unexpected distinction. I am grateful also to my old friend Bob Makin, formerly Director of Radio Vanuatu, for suggesting that I should put my memories of the Condominium on paper, and to Margaret Jolly, ARC Laureate Fellow and Professor at The Australian National University, for recommending their publication and for subsequently giving priority to this task. My very warm thanks are due to Professor Michael Allen, formerly Head of Anthropology, University of Sydney, for editing the memoir. As Michael and I have been friends since meeting in the Condominium when we were quite young men, it is particularly gratifying that he also supported publication. I am grateful to Dr Gregory Rawlings of the University of Otago, and to Professor Howard Van Trease, formerly of the University of the South Pacific, and the University of Hawai'i for their favourable reviews of my manuscript. Lastly, but far from least, my very special thanks to Brian Bresnihan MBE, many years ago my colleague in the New Hebrides British National Service, and friend ever since. Brian has devoted many, many hours to preparing my manuscript for editing and, because I am blind, in reading for me on tape the edited version, together with all the correspondence connected with publication, which would not have been possible without his helpful and wise advice.

Keith Woodward
12 July 2014

A Political Memoir of the Anglo-French Condominium of the New Hebrides

Arrival: Port Vila, Santo and the Condominium

I arrived in the New Hebrides by Qantas flying boat on 26 March 1953. As viewed from the harbour the town could not have looked very different from the Port Vila that Edward Jacomb enthused over upon his arrival on a Burns Philp steamer in 1907.[1] There was no water-front reclamation, Fila Island canoes were drawn up along the beach and the great majority of the buildings were constructed of wood with red or green roofs, many of them being hidden by the luxuriant vegetation.

I had come out from England to take up a junior post at the British Residency (BR). The British Resident Commissioner (BRC) was Brigadier H.J.M. Flaxman, but he was on leave when I arrived and Mr. Bernard Blackwell, an Australian, was acting Resident Commissioner. He had married a sister of the well-known British settler, Geoffrey Seagoe. M. Pierre Anthonioz was then the French Resident Commissioner (FRC) and had moved into a new French Residency (FR) only the year before—into the building which was to become State House, the official residence of the first President of Vanuatu, until it was unfortunately wrecked by Hurricane Uma in 1987. This was a very modern building and quite unlike any other in Port Vila. One witty soul said of it, '*C'est magnifique, mais ce n'est pas la gare*' (It is beautiful, but it is not the railway station)! The BRC lived in splendid isolation at the top of 185 steps on Iririki Island, in a predominantly wooden structure that dated back to 1903.

The British and French judges of the Joint Court were respectively Mr. Anthony Raby-Hieatt and M. Philippe Comte, the Registrar of the Court was M. Edmond Butéri, the Chief Surveyor M. Louis Page and the Registrar of Land Titles was M. Roger Desestre. The Condominium Treasurer was Mr. George S.S. Hill, the Condominium Postmaster Mr. Harold T. Richards, all of whom held their posts for many years (with the exception of the Judges). Mr. Stan Jones was Manager

---

1   Edward Jacomb was an English lawyer who lived in Port Vila during the early years of the Condominium government. His description of Port Vila and surroundings is contained in a microfilm of his unpublished diary which he called 'A Family Portrait' and which is held in the University of London Senate House Library. Copies (Microfilm M 2338) are also held in the National Library of Australia and the State Library of New South Wales. The nine-volume diary spans the years 1899–1923 and his description of Port Vila is contained in Volume 2, Part 1, Chapter 4 titled 'Vila, New Hebrides.' The description was also published in *Nabanga* (the Newsletter of the British Friends of Vanuatu), 2008, issue 98, p. 14.

of Burns Philp (BP) in Port Vila, M. R. Guichard (known as the 'man in the white coat') was Manager of Comptoirs Français des Nouvelles-Hébrides (CFNH), Port Vila and M. Pierre Bourgeois had already established Hébrida (in a building on the seaward side of rue Higginson, the main street of Port Vila, more or less opposite CFNH). M. Antoine Rossi, who was thought by many to resemble closely his fellow Corsican Napoleon Bonaparte, and his wife presided over the hotel of that name, then a very old wooden building.

The principal settler families on Efate were the (French) Colardeaus, the de Gaillandes, Ohlens, the Russets, and (British) Seagoes and Hamlyn-Harrises (the latter at Undine Bay). The former lawyer M. G. Gomichon des Granges ran a fine plantation from his attractive house at Bellevue.

Figure 2. British Paddock with Administration offices.

Source: Photograph by Michael Allen, November 1958

There was, of course, no deep-water wharf in those days and incoming cargo was lightered from the BP steamer *Malaita* and various Messageries Maritimes vessels (of which the elderly *Polynésie* did the regular Sydney, Noumea, New Hebrides run) to the BP and CFNH wharves fronting rue Higginson (Figure 9). Port Vila had enjoyed a town electricity supply provided, as now, by Union Electrique Coloniale des Nouvelles-Hébrides (UNELCO) since 1939, and the mains water system had been completed in 1952 by the Condominium Public

Works Department. Port Vila had a telephone system, the telephone then being of the magneto type, which you would vigorously wind a few times with the handle on the top of the instrument to alert the Exchange, then staffed by Mesdames Benebig and Bouvier and a number of New Hebrideans.

Figure 3. War Memorial, Port Vila, Iririki Island in background.

Source: Photograph by Michael Allen, November 1958.

It was all a far cry from the present-day Port Vila, and even from the one that I left in 1978. Most things had not changed much since the 1930s and there was not much to remind the casual observer that the US forces had garrisoned Port Vila from 1942 onwards, except the large numbers of ex-American Army lorries and jeeps, mainly owned by the planters. The Americans had constructed a fine airfield with a compacted coral runway at Bauerfield, but it was not in use in 1953 as Qantas provided (until 1955) a fortnightly flying-boat service linking Port Vila with Santo, Noumea and Sydney. Although Qantas had given a year's notice of its intention to cease operating the flying-boat by July 1955 because it was uneconomic, the improvements to Bauerfield required by the Australian Department of Civil Aviation (DCA) for Qantas to operate DC4s into it, had not been effected when the service was withdrawn. The French Government considered the DCA's standards to be unnecessarily high. Somewhat more than a year later the French company T.A.I. began a service with DC3s to Port Vila and Santo from Tontouta, New Caledonia, and these aircraft were before long replaced by DC4s. Qantas, however, never resumed its air services to the New Hebrides.

Figure 4. Roman Catholic cathedral, Port Vila.

Source: Photograph by Michael Allen, November 1958.

Figure 5. French Hospital lower-right side, Port Vila.

Source: Photograph by Michael Allen, November 1958.

Figure 6. The Joint Court, Port Vila 1973—formerly the residence of the President of the Court.

Source: Photograph by Brian Bresnihan.

In 1953 Port Vila was still quite a small town. Although the Condominium had recently erected a number of new bungalows, both concrete and wooden, for its staff, and some new private houses had been built in the post-war period, the town had not much changed since the depression years of the 1930s. The main built-up area, bounded on the west by the sea-front road and on the east by the Colardeau plantation, extended from CFNH's D Dock at the southern end of rue Higginson to the area known as Melcoffee (Coffee Mill), where the road leading from the French Hospital (Figure 5) and the main Condominium housing area met the coastal road. The great majority of dwellings were of wooden construction, many of them dating from the early years of the Condominium or before. Apart from those which were installed in the imposing Joint Court building[2] (Survey and Lands Registry) (Figure 6) most of the other Condominium departmental offices were housed, in rather cramped conditions, on the ground floor of what was known as the Condominium building, said to have originally been a hotel. As the Condominium was chronically short of staff quarters, some of its bachelor

---

2 This wooden building was originally the official residence of the President of the Joint Court but when this post was allowed to lapse in 1939, it became available for use as the Joint Court. Unfortunately, this imposing, historic structure was destroyed by fire on 6 June 2007, whether as a result of negligence or arson is not clear.

officers had rooms on the upper floor. This dilapidated building did little credit to public services operated jointly by the world's two greatest colonial powers! It was not to be replaced until the late 1960s by the modern building situated next to the BP store.

Great Britain and France, the two nations which had set up the joint administration of the New Hebrides in 1907, were represented in the territory by Resident Commissioners (RCs), who exercised their powers by delegation from the British and French High Commissioners. In 1953 the residencies were run on pretty much a shoe-string or minimalist basis. The BRC and his small staff of five or six expatriate officers, together with a mixed European and Melanesian clerical staff, occupied an impressive-looking wooden building situated at the top of the British Paddock (now Independence Park) (Figure 2). This structure, built in 1910, was known as the BR or the British Office. The BRC lived, however, in the BR house on Iririki. In 1953 he was still taken from the island to the Customs jetty on the mainland in a rowing boat manned by two or more Melanesians, known as the 'boat boys', who wore the sailor's uniform traditional to British matelots. The British District Agent for Central District No. 1 (CD1), who was then also British Commandant of Police, had an office in the Police/Prison compound a little way across the Paddock.

There appears to have been a gentleman's agreement between the British and French Residencies, dating presumably from the early years of the Condominium, that the two national flags would be flown at the same level. Not having been told of this, I was somewhat surprised when—probably in 1954—M. Jean-Marie Jouve, the Chancelier (the No. 2 to the FRC) at the FR, telephoned to enquire whether we in the BR would have any objection to the *Tricouleur* being flown from a pole situated on higher ground than the Union flag. He explained that this was a consequence of the FR having been re-sited on land higher up the town—in 1952 as mentioned earlier. Despite my very junior position, and without even thinking of consulting my superiors, I answered that of course we didn't mind. The new FR in fact directly overlooked the British compound, and enjoyed a spectacular view of the harbour, Iririki, Fila Island and the two headlands of Pango and Devil's Point.

It seems that up to that point, the official French flagpole had remained at the site of the old Residency, which was very close to the War Memorial (Figure 3) and the old Joint Court. It was on this site that the French Administration erected a new secretariat building in the early 1960s. This building is now occupied by the Prime Minister and various departmental offices. Prior to its construction, the Chancelier and other French officials had worked in premises separate from the FR building in which the FRC had his private office or *cabinet*, as well as his living quarters.

Before transferring in 1952 to the new Residency, the FRC and his personal secretariat had occupied an old wooden structure which stood on the site where the building, now used by the Prime Minister and other Vanuatu Government ministers, was erected in the mid-1960s as a new FR-combined Secretariat. In the intervening period the old FR, built at the beginning of the twentieth century, was used as a school. The new Residency, into which the FRC had moved by 1953, stood on high ground overlooking the British Paddock and affording a splendid view of the harbour and Devil's Point beyond. The Chancelier, or counterpart to the British Assistant RC, and the remainder of the French Secretariat occupied an elderly building behind the old Joint Court. The latter, which was demolished in the early 1970s, had stood on a site immediately above the War Memorial. The staff of the FR was comparable in size to that of the BR. The FR, however, filled its clerical posts with European women, owing to the lack, at that period, of suitably educated Melanesians, together with the need to provide employment for locally domiciled Frenchwomen, as was explained to me by a high-ranking French official, M. L'Inspecteur Sanner, who visited Port Vila in 1954.

No cruise ships visited the New Hebrides in the 1950s, and there was virtually no tourism. The economy of the Condominium was overwhelmingly based on the export of copra with Melanesian production soon to match, and later overtake, that from European (mainly French) plantations. The world copra price was very high in the early 1950s, owing to the Korean War, and the New Hebrides was enjoying a period of prosperity. In 1952, one planter on Efate was said to have made £20,000 Australian, then a huge sum. Melanesians too benefited from the good copra price, and from high wages on the plantations. By 1953, exports of the more labour-intensive cash crops cacao and coffee, which, together with cotton, had once been important, had shrunk to a few hundred tons. The starting of the tuna fishing industry, based at Palekula, Santo was still four years into the future (1957), but the local entrepreneur, Mr. Donald J. Gubbay, was already making plans for it, in conjunction with a Japanese company. In 1953, however, commerce in the New Hebrides, especially the buying and exporting of copra and the selling of imported merchandise throughout the islands, was dominated by the long-established Australian firm of BP of Sydney, and CFNH owned by the Ballandes of Bordeaux and Nouméa. Chinese shopkeepers in Luganville, Santo, as well as in Port Vila, had an important part of the local retail trade, and were much patronised by Melanesians, perhaps because, so I heard, they had to wait while Europeans were served first in European stores.

Figure 7. Burns Philp's pier and Iririki Island on right.

Source: Photograph by Michael Allen, November 1958.

In the 1950s, there were still no locally operated air services in the Condominion. Moreover, the withdrawal by Qantas in July 1955 of its flying boat service from Sydney and Noumea meant that the New Hebrides had no air link with the outside world until the French airline, TAI, instituted a service between Port Vila, Santo and Noumea in 1956. During that period, communication between the islands depended entirely on local shipping, with both BP and Ballandes operating inter-island trading vessels together with a few local businessmen (Figure 7). In January 1956, I had the pleasure of a leisurely voyage from Santo to Port Vila on BP's trading schooner, *Moala*, much of it under sail when the wind was favourable; a delightful Fijian seaman, the late Osea Tunidau, was in command, with a Melanesian crew. I had travelled to Santo on the new BP ship, the *MV Tulagi*, which had just come on to the Sydney, New Hebrides and New Guinea line.

In 1953, we had no accurate figure for the population of the New Hebrides, but it is a fairly safe guess that it was about 60,000, since it had reached some 78,000 by the time of the 1967 census. The overwhelming majority was Melanesian with up to 1,500, mainly French, European, rather more than 2,000 Vietnamese (known then as Tonkinese) and a few hundred Chinese.[3] There were also some dozens of Wallis Island plantation workers.

Figure 8. Keith Woodward and unidentified friend at one of Port Vila's nearby beaches.

Source: Photograph by Michael Allen, November 1958.

Members of the predominantly French European community on Santo rather resented being governed from Port Vila and were apt to point out that much more copra was either produced on, or exported through, Santo from other northern islands than was handled in Port Vila. This fact was recognised by the Condominium authorities when Santo was given priority over Port Vila for the construction of a deep-water wharf (completed in 1958), the largest civil

---

3 In the early 1920s the French Government had arranged for Vietnamese to be brought to the New Hebrides to relieve the chronic shortage of labour on French-owned plantations. By 1953, however, most of the Tonkinese (as they were then usually called, from the province of Indo-China where they had originated) had left the plantations, and had become artisans, taxi-drivers, barbers, market-gardeners or domestic servants. They were technically *en instance de rapatriment* (awaiting repatriation) to their homeland, but the Vietminh insurgency in French Indo-China, which led in 1954 to North Vietnam becoming an independent state, resulted in their return being delayed. It was not until 1963 that the majority of the Tonkinese left the New Hebrides. Whilst the older ones among them wanted to go back to Vietnam, many, or most of the Vietnamese who had been born in the Condominium went reluctantly, and in some cases hid themselves to avoid being taken to a country to which they felt no attachment. Some 300 Vietnamese were able to remain in the New Hebrides.

engineering project so far financed by the Joint Administration. I had been told that the settlement situated on the northern side of the Segond Channel (often referred to as 'the canal' in those days) was very different, both physically and in its whole atmosphere, from Port Vila. I was immediately struck, visiting Luganville for the first time in December 1954, by this difference. Whereas Port Vila, apart from being much larger, was a compact town, Luganville (the name was, however, not much used in Port Vila then) was strung along a few miles of the south coast of Santo, beginning in the west with the French District Agency, the French Hospital and the Catholic Mission. Going eastwards, one came to the Condominium Radio Station, and further on, BP's main store. It was, however, on the east side of the Sarakata River that the main commercial area was to be found—Chinese stores (Fung Kwan Chee's, Ah Yuen's and Johnny Lum's), Desplat's Garage, the Hotel Corsica, various bars, the cinema and CFNH—I forget in which order. The main street (also named rue Higginson) was quite wide—a relic of the US wartime presence, as were all the roads in the area, and the numerous Quonset huts. There was, some people said, a 'wild west' atmosphere about the place, and that was my impression. It was certainly reminiscent of some small American mid-West towns, and one would not have been surprised to see a cowboy hitch his horse to a tethering-rail outside one of the bars. The British District Agency was then still situated on the small island of Venue, off the south-west coast, but the District Agent had a town office and sleeping accommodation in the ex-US Navy PT Base, on the Sarakata River. The Condominium Customs and Survey Departments may also have had offices in the Base buildings.

Figure 9. The *Polynésie*, from the Rossi Hotel, Port Vila waterfront.

Source: Photograph by Michael Allen, November 1958.

When I arrived in the New Hebrides in 1953 nothing was happening regarding its political future, nor did it seem likely that anything would, at least not in the foreseeable future. The Anglo-French Condominium system of government had been in existence for a little over forty-five years and, as far as anyone could see, looked set to go on indefinitely. Some visitors, especially Australian journalists, were inclined to laugh at the Condominium with its two police forces wearing quaint and quite different uniforms, and called it the Pandemonium. However, no one was talking publicly about changing it. In the years immediately following the Great War of 1914–18, the British and French Governments had looked at possible alternatives to the continuation of the Condominium, such as partition of the group between the two Powers, or one of them making way for the other, to be compensated, perhaps by an African colony. Given the serious difficulties involved in the adoption of either of these options, it was found much easier to continue with the *status quo*, and in 1922, the Anglo-French Protocol of 6 August 1914, which had been suspended because of the outbreak of war with Germany, had duly been brought into force.

There was, moreover, no agitation for change in the New Hebrides in 1953, either among the small European communities, or the Melanesian population. The copra price was still high, and Melanesians could earn good wages. The abuses that had attended their employment on plantations in the early years of the Condominium were a thing of the past, and many planters had standing arrangements with particular villages for the supply of labour. No major hurricane or earthquake had hit Port Vila for many years, and in the group as a whole the most serious recent natural disaster had been a combination of earthquake and hurricane damage on Ambrym in 1950–51, which resulted in the re-settlement on French-owned land near Mele village, Efate, of people from Maat on Ambrym. Their new village was usually known as Mele-Maat, or just Maat.

At this period, there had been no extensive migration to Port Vila of people from the outer islands, although there were some small groups from the islands living in the peri-urban area as, for example, people from Pentecost at Tebakor, just north of Port Vila, who had their own Anglican church on land owned by a Fila Island family. Some years later, I was to be much involved in helping these people re-locate to the Anglican Church land at Tagabe. This was bought from Harry Ohlen at the very reasonable price of one shilling and three pence Australian a square metre (AU12.5 cents). That was in 1959, long before the era of land speculation.

Relations between the British and French Residencies, both at work and socially, were good when I arrived in Port Vila. At that particular time, there were no matters at issue that involved any significant divergence in policy between the two sides of the Condominium. The FRC, Pierre Anthonioz, who had had a remarkable military career with the Free French during World War II, was very sociable, and the officers of the BR and their wives enjoyed much lavish hospitality at the FR, where the champagne flowed. Anthonioz was a good swimmer, despite having a crippled right arm, the result of a war wound, and not long before my arrival had swum between Pango and Devil's Point, a distance of approximately 6.2 miles (10 kilometres). At this time, the staff of the two Residencies were quite small, and this fact gave rise to more social contacts between them than I recall from later years, when both staffs were much larger, and socially more self-sufficient.

Relations with New Hebrideans

Although there was no explicit colour bar directed against Melanesians, it could not be said that Europeans and Melanesians lived on an equal footing in the 1950s. One did not, for example, expect to find Melanesians drinking or dining in the Hotel Rossi. There was virtually no social contact in Port Vila between Europeans and Melanesians, although the chiefs of the villages around the town were invited to the large receptions given by the two Residencies on occasions such as the Queen's Birthday, the 14th July, and the visits of High Commissioners or other important persons. I was often addressed as *Masta* when encountering a Melanesian. The planters, and many other people, usually referred to male Melanesian labourers as 'boys'. The living quarters provided by BP for their labour were a disgrace. It is not without a sense of shame, moreover, that I remember the sub-standard housing provided by the BR for its Melanesian clerical staff—all corrugated iron huts with no modern toilet or washing facilities, minimal furniture, and, of course, no refrigerators or proper cookers (which, in any case, their low salaries would not have enabled them to use; the cost of electricity, kerosene and white spirit being very high).

In the 1950s, the legal status of the indigenous New Hebrideans (I shall use this term henceforth, though it should be noted that since 1980 indigenous New Hebrideans have been known as ni-Vanuatu) was not a matter of discontent on their part. When in the following decade, New Hebrideans began to travel beyond the south-west Pacific, their lack of a proper passport sometimes caused difficulties, as immigration officials were not familiar with the unimpressive identity card, bearing the signatures of both Resident Commissioners, carried by New Hebrideans. The statelessness of New Hebrideans became an issue in the Advisory Council (AdCo), and the Resident Commissioners promised to provide New Hebrideans with a travel document which looked like a normal passport. The Resident Commissioners were powerless to do more, as New Hebrideans could not be citizens of a state which did not exist, or of a colonial territory that was not a legal entity.

In my view, the only inequality suffered by New Hebrideans from a judicial system otherwise fair to them was the failure of the Protocol to provide for New Hebrideans to sit as Assessors on the Joint Court and the Courts of First Instance (the latter dealt with offences against Joint Regulations) when New Hebrideans appeared before these courts. I was instrumental in getting this defect remedied, but only a few years before Independence. In general, I found the sentencing in all the courts, and especially the Joint Court, to be light.

I suppose the most charitable term that one can apply to the attitude of most Europeans, and of Government, towards the indigenous people of the group is paternalism. The inequalities of status which went with paternalism are perhaps best illustrated by the fact that, among the various races inhabiting the New Hebrides, the Melanesians were legally prohibited from consuming alcohol by the Protocol of 1914. This prohibition, which doubtless owed much to mission influence, was intended for the good of the people subjected to it. Unfortunately, however, it could not be thoroughly enforced. Many New Hebrideans succeeded in obtaining liquor, as plantation owners found it easier to obtain labour if they supplied it. There were, moreover, not a few traders operating in the outer islands, who could make good profits from flouting the prohibitions on the sale of liquor to New Hebrideans, and hardly any were ever prosecuted. Nor was prohibition strictly enforced on New Hebrideans, unless they were discovered by the police, drunk and incapable or disorderly, in a public place. This meant in practice that New Hebrideans were only prosecuted in Port Vila and Luganville, since there was virtually no police presence in the rural areas. In the two towns, however, the District Agents displayed a certain amount of energy, especially on Saturday evenings, in looking for drunks. Apart from the desirability of letting the hapless offenders sober up out of harm's way in the *kalabus* (prison),[4] a good round up of drunks at the weekend would ensure the availability of labour for grass-cutting during the following week. The sentence usually handed down by the courts for ordinary cases of public inebriety was one week inside.

The liquor prohibition could give rise to social embarrassment. If I was attending, say a Queen's Birthday reception at the BR, and talking to one of the chiefs, or a New Hebridean medical officer, I felt uneasy to be holding a glass of beer, whilst he could have only lemonade. It has to be acknowledged, however, that New Hebridean guests often left these functions somewhat under the weather, as the Residency bar-tenders, themselves Melanesians, connived at discreet infringement of the liquor law! Who could blame them? The BRC did not worry unduly, provided no one got obviously and embarrassingly tipsy. Prohibition was relaxed in 1962, when it was agreed by the Advisory Council that New Hebrideans should be allowed to buy beer and wine, but not drink in bars. The ban on their consumption of spirits was not lifted, however, until 1974 (at the last but one session of AdCo).

Domestic and public architecture

Although I had got married in London on 7 March 1953, I arrived in Port Vila alone, as my wife, Joyce, had to work out her three months' notice before leaving her secretarial post at St. Mary's Hospital, Paddington to join me. So I was billeted with my old Oxford friend Michael Challons and his Swedish wife Barbara, who then occupied BR house No. 3. This large wooden bungalow had been built (with two others of the same design) in 1909. Edward Jacomb had been the first occupant of it. House No. 3 stood outside the British Paddock, on a beautiful site, with large shade trees in a long garden that ended at the top of the cliff overlooking the Condominium workshops (their site is now occupied by the Government office building) and the BP store. The old Presbyterian Church (destroyed completely in the 1959 hurricane) was situated immediately opposite the house, just a few yards from our front entrance. This fine old house, so suitable for tropical living, which had withstood the hurricane, was demolished

---

4   Kalabus is the Bislama word for a prison and in common use in the New Hebrides and now Vanuatu.

in the late 1960s, when the site was transferred to Condominium ownership for the construction of a concrete house for a head of department. When I re-visited Port Vila with my second wife Elizabeth in 1988 we were guests for dinner there of Home Affairs Minister, Sethy Regenvanu and his wife, Dorothy.

When I walked up the middle road of the British Paddock on 27 March 1953 to begin work at the British office, the landscape was very different from the present-day one. There were fewer houses to be seen, many more coconut palms, as well as three large shade trees, which stood on the northern side of the Paddock, in front of the house now occupied by the Prime Minister. There was long grass on this side of the Paddock and this provided grazing for the small herd of horses which then roamed around in it. My old bungalow, which was also located in this area of the Paddock, has long been replaced by the Melanesian Spearhead headquarters building.[5] Across the cricket field on the other side could be seen the building of the British Police and the British Prison.

Standing in relative isolation southward of the cricket field was a wooden building, the British School. This one-classroom establishment took the children of BR staff, including New Hebrideans, and also of British and Australian people in the commercial sector, the Condominium and the Presbyterian Mission, at junior primary level. In 1953, the teacher in charge was Mrs. Ruth Peebles, the wife of one of my colleagues. A few years later, this school was demolished, and replaced by a larger one, in the building which now houses the offices of the Ministry of Education. The cost of running the Paddock School and a subsidy of £200 per annum to the Presbyterian Mission's Iririki District School (situated, despite its name, on the road to Pango Point), constituted the totality of the British Government expenditure on education in those days.

Constitutional advance?

In 1953, the New Hebrides may have been almost alone among British and French colonial territories in not having any kind of representative institution. There was, however, no political pressure from within the Anglo-French Condominium for the establishment of some kind of representative body. There was no agitation for constitutional advance, and the population at large seemed content with their unique form of administration by two nations. No doubt people would have liked to see more infrastructural and social development, such as more and better roads, schools and health services. On the other hand, taxation was light (there was no income or corporation tax) and the Government

---

5   The Melanesian Spearhead Group (MSG) is a governmental organisation consisting of the four Melanesian states of Fiji, Papua New Guinea, Solomon Islands, Vanuatu and the Kanak and Socialist National Liberation Front of New Caledonia. It was founded as a political organisation in 1983.

did not impinge much on the everyday lives of the Condominium's inhabitants. This was particularly true of the great majority of the Melanesian population living in the rural areas. Unless they committed more than minor crimes, or engaged in some kind of activity that the RCs deemed subversive, most New Hebridean villagers could simply ignore the *Gavman* (Bislama for Government).

Having just alluded to subversive activity, it is convenient to digress briefly from the question of constitutional advance, or lack of it, in order to mention the John Frum movement. This movement, a kind of millenarian 'cult', started up on Tanna in the early 1940s. In 1953, its principal leaders were either still in prison or exiled from Tanna, or recently had been. At this stage, the Joint Administration was pursuing a policy of repression towards this movement. This was, however, to change after 1957, to be replaced by toleration, on the understanding impressed on Nakomaha (a leader of the movement) and his fellow John Frum bosses by the RCs in person that they did not impinge upon the lives of non-cult villages.[6]

My personal contact with John Frum was virtually nil. I did visit Ipekel with the then British District Agent, Southern District, Michael Challons, in May 1957, but our brief conversation with Mwailes and other John Frum notables unsurprisingly gave us no indication that they were planning to march around Tanna, the episode which caused such concern some weeks later. I thought their demeanour towards Challons at this encounter was, although not actually hostile, one of indifference, and far removed from the usual courteous friendliness experienced by district agents when visiting New Hebridean villages. Challons had a very good way with New Hebrideans and made himself very popular during his three years or so on Tanna.

The absence in the New Hebrides of any representative body should be viewed in a world-wide and, especially, in a Pacific context. Though France and Great Britain had endorsed the principle of self-determination in the Atlantic Charter in 1941 they still had large colonial empires, and with very few exceptions, none was on the point of gaining independence. This was particularly true in the South Pacific. The British Solomon Islands had only a nominated Advisory Council, and the Gilbert (Kiribati) and Ellice Islands Colony (Tuvalu) had not even this modest form of representation. The French territories of New Caledonia and French Polynesia had elected assemblies, but the executive powers were firmly in the hands of their governors. In the New Hebrides at this

---

6 Soon after the release of Nakomaha from prison very early in 1957, the men of the principal John Frum village of Ipekel, Sulphur Bay, began drilling with wooden muskets. When, a few months later they began marching into non-John Frum districts, adopting a somewhat menacing posture, both RCs visited Ipekel with a joint police detachment, collected up the wooden muskets, and made it clear that such activities would not be countenanced. Marching outside Sulphur Bay was, in fact, never resumed and nor were any John Frum leaders imprisoned.

time, the indigenous people were in no way politicised, and there was, as yet, no sign of awakening political awareness. Only a very small number had received any kind of secondary education and, importantly, there were no Melanesian university graduates. People did not read newspapers, and the era of generalised ownership of transistor radios had not yet arrived. The preoccupations of rural New Hebrideans were not what was going on in the outside world, but with their churches, the state of their subsistence gardens and the price of copra.

In 1953, despite the absence of any pressure in the New Hebrides for constitutional advance, the important people concerned with such matters must have decided that something should be done to initiate progress, even if only slowly and modestly. Given my own very junior position in the BR, I was, of course, quite unaware of what was brewing until late in that year, or the beginning of 1954, so I do not know whether the opening move for 'doing something about the New Hebrides' came from London or Paris.

A conference to consider the future of the New Hebrides was held in Honiara, the capital of the British Solomon Islands Protectorate, in March 1954. It was attended by the British High Commissioner for the western Pacific, Sir Robert Stanley, by his French counterpart, M. Angamarre, by the BRC, Mr. (later Sir) Hubert Flaxman and by his French colleague, M. Pierre Anthonioz. A high-ranking official from Paris, M. L'Inspecteur Sanner, was also present. I do not remember whether the British Colonial Office was represented at the meeting, but I think not. This conference was important in the history of the Condominium because it showed that the British and French Governments, long content to let the New Hebrides be a colonial backwater, where no progress took place, realised that the time had come for change. The need to promote economic development was recognised, and the decision to build the deep-water wharf at Santo was almost certainly taken at this conference together with some minor administrative changes concerning Condominium public services. The major decisions, however, and the only ones that concern us here, were of a constitutional nature. The High Commissioners decided to recommend to their respective Governments the setting up of an Advisory Council, and of an embryonic system of local government, both of which were to involve a degree of popular representation in the conduct of public affairs.

The Advisory Council—AdCo

It was not until 1957 that a Joint Regulation was made to establish a temporary Advisory Council for the New Hebrides (JRs were the form of legislation used in the Condominium and were usually signed by the two RCs). Most unusually, it was signed by the British and French High Commissioners, and I was present in the BRC's office when Sir John Gutch, who had succeeded Stanley as High Commissioner in 1955, signed the English and French texts (all Condominium legislation was, of course, issued in both languages). The JR provided for an Advisory Council composed of four British, four French and four New Hebridean unofficial private members, together with two official members and the RCs, who were to be the joint Presidents. The two official members were always the Condominium Treasurer and the Superintendent of Public Works, these posts being held, invariably by a British and French official respectively. The Council, usually known as AdCo, had no legislative power and its function was to advise the RCs on the matters (which had to include the Condominium budget) referred to it. Although, in practice, the RCs consulted AdCo on most important matters, it was not always possible to do so as the Council only met, primarily to examine the proposed Condominium budget, once a year for the first few years after its inception in 1958. Exceptionally, however, there were two sessions in 1958—an inaugural one at the beginning of the year, and the Budget Session at the end of it.

The first few sessions of AdCo were held in the audience chamber of the old Joint Court, but its meetings took place in the Port Vila Cultural Centre after completion of the Centre in 1960 or 1961. In the early days of AdCo we did not have simultaneous interpretation facilities, which were acquired only after the Council began meeting in the long hall of the Cultural Centre, where there was enough space for the installation of the interpreters' booths. While the AdCo sessions were still held in the old Joint Court, proceedings were considerably slowed down by consecutive interpretation, with M. Louis Page (the Chief Surveyor) and a bilingual officer from the BR translating each speech, sentence by sentence after the person speaking, into French or English. In addition, as some of the New Hebridean members did not understand either of these languages, translation into Bislama also had to be provided, usually by M. Raymond Colardeau (a younger brother of the planter, M. Andre Colardeau). I attended all the AdCo sittings in the capacity of Secretary, in order to take summarised notes of the speeches, as we did not then make a verbatim record of the debates (that was begun when we had simultaneous interpretation). After being put into shape by dictation to my secretary, and approved by my French colleague, my summary of the proceedings became the official record, and was in due course distributed to AdCo members. I very much wish that I had kept copies of these early AdCo minutes, as I fear it would now be difficult, if not impossible, to locate any of them in Vanuatu.

Up until 1964, the members of AdCo were appointed jointly by the RCs, with each RC nominating, for his colleague's agreement, the members of his own nationality and half of the New Hebridean ones. It was the unwritten convention that the RCs accepted each other's nominations without demur. Among the earliest

British AdCo members, as far as I can recall, were R.U. Paul of Tanna; G. Wilson, Manager of BP, Port Vila; the Reverend R.W. Murray, Presbyterian missionary from Nguna; and Keith Solway, a Santo planter. The French members were Monseigneur Julliard, the Catholic Bishop; R. Guichard, Manager of CFNH, Port Vila; H. Ohlen, planter, Efate; and Jean My, planter, Santo. The New Hebrideans were Dr. John Kalsakau, Fila Island; John Qarani, Vanua Lava; Thomas Noal, Port Resolution, Tanna; Chief Jack of Pinalum, Malekula; and Chief Toma Avusa later named Tom Tiploamata of Tongoa. None of these was francophone, as it was very difficult in those days for the FR to find French-speaking Melanesians of a status appropriate for AdCo membership. Ex-President of Vanuatu, Jean-Marie Leyhe, was, I think, the first francophone AdCo member.

The RCs also appointed an alternate member for each full AdCo member. Alternate members took the place of full members when they were unable to attend sessions of the Council. Mr. Ken Hutton, then resident at Luganville, was Keith Solway's alternate, and he attended far more meetings of AdCo than Solway, who seemed little interested in making any contribution to the Council's work. I think we gained by the exchange, as Hutton took an active and useful part in the proceedings.

When writing of the first meeting of AdCo, I was reminded of a tragic incident that occurred in 1952 on a plantation in the Big Bay area of Santo. A French plantation manager called Chavreau shot dead two men from the Santo Bush, who were working on the plantation, because—he alleged—one of them struck, or threatened him. Chavreau was given a suspended sentence of one year's imprisonment. The double killing aroused intense resentment among the bush people, who withdrew their labour from European plantations for some years. As part of the measures recommended by the French anthropologist, Jean Guiart (Figure 11), to restore confidence among the bush villagers, one of their leading big men, Mol Valivu, was brought down to Port Vila to sit in on the inaugural session of AdCo. Other measures taken by the FR at Guiart's suggestion included the setting up of a school and a co-operative for Mol Valivu's people at Ipayato, south-west Santo. These various remedial measures had a good effect, and I recall being escorted by Mol Valivu for part of our walk into the Santo high country in May 1958, when I was a member of a small party of officials investigating a disputed prospecting licence claim, involving Mr. D.J. Gubbay and the French mining company, CFPO. We settled the dispute amicably.

In 1959, the New Hebridean membership of AdCo was increased from four to eight. Thus was instituted the principle, not to be abandoned until 1974, of parity of membership between New Hebridean native and non-native members. Although this parity was obviously incompatible with the enormous disparity between the Melanesian and non-native populations, it was considered at the time that the contribution made by the small European community to the economy was some justification for its disproportionate representation on AdCo. The disparity was apparently accepted with good grace by the New Hebridean AdCo members, and the early sessions were quiet affairs. At this stage, the European members did most of the talking, their interventions being mainly concerned with various Heads of the Budget as they related to their own local concerns.

The road to self-government

By 1963, we in the BR were thinking that it was time to take a further step, even if only a small one, along the road which would ultimately lead the New Hebrides to self-government. It was, I suppose, natural that we should take account of what was going on in the Solomon Islands, a neighbouring British territory, which was also peopled by Melanesians, and was at a stage of development comparable to that of the New Hebrides. In 1960, or soon afterwards, the Solomons, which had had an AdCo since 1928, had been given a Legislative Council (known as LegCo for short). It should not be thought, however, that the establishment of LegCo marked a momentous degree of constitutional advance. The Council contained only four private members, two European and two Solomon Islanders, all appointed by the High Commissioner, who presided at its sittings. There were also five official members, who held the most senior posts in the Government. Since these constituted a majority of the Council, the Government was always sure of getting its legislation passed, even if all the private members opposed it. In 1963, the BRC sent me to Honiara for a few days, so that I could sit in on a session of LegCo, to see how it functioned.

The private members of LegCo were then the Anglican Bishop of Melanesia, the Right Reverend Alfred Hill; a European businessman called Lawson; Anglican Assistant Bishop Leonard Alufarai (of Malaita); and Methodist Minister, Wesley Cary, also a Solomon Islander. From my point of view, the most interesting thing that occurred while I attended the sittings happened when the four private members tabled a motion proposing that there should be a member of LegCo elected by universal suffrage to represent Honiara. The four members duly spoke in support of their motion, but it was not acceptable to the Government. I thought the High Commissioner, Sir David Trench, displayed a certain lack of regard for due parliamentary procedure, to say nothing of tact, when after the four private members had voted for the motion, he did not bother to ask the officials to vote, but simply announced from the Chair that their motion was lost! I was Bishop Hill's guest for dinner that evening, and he and Bishop Leonard were in a very anti-Administration mood, because of the cavalier way in which their motion had been treated. I shared their feelings and said so.

My attendance at the session of the Solomons LegCo had been an instructive and useful experience. I returned to Port Vila convinced that we in the New Hebrides should not, on our way to ultimate self-government, go through the stage of a legislature with an official majority, which I felt to be (from a democratic viewpoint) valueless. In reality, the private members of the Honiara LegCo had no more power than had the members of the preceding AdCo. Their views could be over-ruled whenever the High Commissioner chose to bring the big guns of his official majority to bear on them. Moreover, I thought our French colleagues were too logical to see any point in such a contrived constitutional device, to say nothing of the people of the New Hebrides.

Although, at this time—the early 1960s—there was no popular pressure on the New Hebrides Joint Administration for further constitutional advance, I believed that only a few years would elapse before we faced demands for such advance, as progress in the education of New Hebrideans brought an educated élite into being. I was also aware that there were those among the European community, who thought they should have some influence on the conduct of public affairs. In settling out my ideas on the subject to the RC (then Mr. A.M. Wilkie, CMG) and Mr. (later Sir) Michael Gass, then Chief Secretary to the Western Pacific High Commission, I stressed the desirability of keeping ahead of political pressure by bringing in the next stage of constitutional advance, without waiting for popular demand to build up. I said that if we pursued this policy we would be better able to manage progress towards self-government at a pace commensurate with the readiness of the people for it. In this way, the Joint Administration might perhaps avoid being hustled precipitately into an advanced state of self-government for the territory, without having prepared the way for it by passing through a gradual process of evolution. In the event, of course, what I hoped to avoid was what happened, as a result of the French Government being unwilling to move the Condominium beyond the AdCo stage, as we shall see, until 1975, by which time the National Party (NP) was clamouring for independence.

To return to 1964—I was then authorised, in my capacity as a kind of political adviser, to approach the FR at Chancelier level, in order to ascertain our colleagues' views on some further constitutional advance. The FRC at that time was M. Maurice Delauney (1961–64) who, after a varied career, died in December 2009 at the age of ninety. The Chancelier was M. Robert Langlois. Perhaps inspired by the motion of the private members of the Solomons LegCo in 1963, I suggested to Langlois that some members of AdCo should be elected by universal suffrage to represent Port Vila and Luganville. Langlois gave me a courteous and attentive hearing and said the FR would consider that suggestion. Nothing came of it, however, and I am now rather doubtful as to the validity of singling out one or both towns for an advanced dose of democracy. The main argument for so doing was that it would have been fairly easy to organise direct elections in the urban areas, as compared with the islands.

In the meantime, things had moved on in the Solomons, where LegCo was to have a number of members elected by the Local Councils that covered the whole of the Protectorate. This seemed an arrangement that could be extended to the New Hebrides. We therefore proposed to the FR that the number of AdCo private members should be increased from sixteen to twenty (ten New Hebrideans and ten expatriates), and that four members in each category should be indirectly elected.

Beginning in 1957 some Local Councils, which exercised authority only over Melanesians, had been set up. It appeared to me feasible that representatives of Local Councils should meet together in each of the four Districts, and should elect a member of AdCo. This would be a modest step forward. Given the small size of the non-native population, it would have been fairly easy for it to elect four AdCo members by direct suffrage, but this would have been invidious, as it would have accorded a greater degree of democracy to the non-natives than to the New Hebrideans. The Chamber of Commerce provided the solution to our problems.

The New Hebrides Chamber of Commerce, Industry and Agriculture, established by Joint Regulation in 1963, had an electoral college composed mainly, or entirely, of non-natives, principally Europeans. However, half of the actual members of the Chamber were appointed by the RCs, and these included a number of New Hebrideans, such as André Carlot of Erakor, to ensure that the commercial interests of Melanesians were not overlooked. It seemed to me in 1964 that the Chamber of Commerce Electoral College of some 230 persons would be a suitable body of people for the purpose of electing four non-native AdCo Members.[7] This device for the choice of non-native members would, I thought, constitute an unobjectionable counterpart to the Local Council electoral colleges proposed for getting four New Hebrideans indirectly elected to AdCo.

The BRC, Mr. A.M. Wilkie, approved my proposals, and these were submitted to the FR, which accepted them quite happily. The second AdCo set up in 1964 had twenty-six members, six more than the 1959 body. It was composed of twenty private members, eight of whom were indirectly elected, the two RCs, Joint Presidents, two Condominium Heads of Department, and (an innovation) the British Assistant RC, then Mr. (later Sir) Colin Allan,[8] and the Chancelier of the FR, M. Robert Langlois.

---

7   Persons holding a trading licence were eligible for inclusion in the Chamber of Commerce Electoral College.
8   Later, upon Mr. Wilkie's death in 1966, Allan became BRC. Leaving the New Hebrides in 1973, he became the last Governor of the Seychelles, and then the last Governor of the British Solomon Islands Protectorate, which gained its independence in 1978. He died in Auckland in 1993.

The enlarged, and partly-elected AdCo, which began its life in 1964, remained a purely advisory body. However, the RCs sought to counteract the Council's lack of formal deliberative powers by submitting all important proposals for legislation, and other weighty matters, such as the Joint Development Plan, to it for consideration. To this end, the Council was usually convened for a mid-year session, in addition to the end of year budget meeting. Moreover, if proposed Joint Regulations or other matters were deemed sufficiently urgent to make it undesirable to defer them until the next AdCo full session, they would be referred to the Council's Standing Committee, which, because it was much smaller, could be convened more quickly and at less expense. As I recall it, the Standing Committee was composed of eight private members (four New Hebrideans and four Europeans) and four of the six official members, including, of course, the two RCs as joint chairmen.

As the 1960s wore on members of AdCo, and more especially the New Hebridean and British ones, began to press for more rapid constitutional advance, while behind the scenes the British Government was seeking French agreement for the replacement of AdCo by a legislative body. These negotiations were, however, uphill work, as the French Government remained to be convinced that the New Hebrideans were yet 'politically mature' enough for such a change. From an objective viewpoint this may well have been true, since the New Hebridean people had enjoyed only a very brief and inadequate involvement in the conduct, at the national level, of public affairs. Experience in her colonial empire worldwide had, however, taught Britain that once a colonised people began to think it had the right to run its own affairs, such feelings quickly gathered momentum, and could not long be held in check by recourse to objective criteria as to the readiness, or otherwise, of that people for self-government. Indeed, events in the New Hebrides during the 1970s bore witness yet again to this inescapable truth.

The FR got a shock when, on Joan of Arc Day, in June 1966, the recently ordained Roman Catholic priest, Fr. Gérard Leymang, in a sermon preached to a congregation which included the two RCs, alluded to the prospect of the New Hebrides one day becoming independent. Father Charles Verlingue subsequently called upon the BRC to apologise, on behalf of the Bishop (Monseigneur Julliard) for Gérard's untimely gaffe. He was assured by Mr. Wilkie that no apology was necessary. Shortly afterwards, the erring cleric was sent off to the Catholic University at Lyon, France, to pursue a two-year course in social studies. Exile did not diminish Leymang's interest in public affairs in the New Hebrides, and it fell to me to answer letters from him to the BR seeking information relevant to political development. There was, perhaps, some significance in his choosing to write to us, despite being a francophone. After Leymang's return from Lyon the FR very sensibly made him a member of AdCo. In this capacity he was quite forthright in criticism of the Joint Administration and in pressing for constitutional advance. Leymang was an early member of the NP, but he found a more congenial political home in the Union des Communautés des Nouvelles-

Hébrides (UCNH) later on. The NP (subsequently renamed the Vanuaku Party/ Vanu'aki Pati) might possibly have attracted other radical francophones had it not, by virtue of injudicious pronouncements at various times, conveyed the impression that it posed a threat to French education, and the interests of francophone New Hebrideans.

What I recall most clearly about the second AdCo in 1964–69, is not so much pressure from members for constitutional change (which was to be much greater in the third Council), but the emergence of the land question as the foremost issue of the political scene.

The land question

During the last quarter of the nineteenth century, there was very extensive purchasing of land by Europeans, and especially by the agents of the company which, in 1894, became the Société Française des Nouvelles-Hébrides (SFNH), and particularly on the islands of Espiritu Santo, Malekula, Epi and Efate. By the time of the establishment in 1910 of the Joint Court (a primary function of which was to adjudicate land claims), applications lodged with it by European companies and individuals covered at least one-third of the total area of the New Hebrides. Many plantations had been created on the basis of these claims early in the twentieth century, long before the Joint Court was able to begin hearing land claims in 1927.

In the last decade or two of the nineteenth and the first two or three of the twentieth centuries, when European cotton and coconut plantations were being created, the indigenous population of the New Hebrides was either still in decline, or had barely begun its slow recovery. The effective alienation of land represented by these plantations did not, therefore, bring about shortages of cultivable land for most Melanesian villages. In 1953, land did not appear to be an important or urgent issue between New Hebrideans and Europeans. In the Port Vila area, however, the peri-urban villages of Fila Island, now known as Ifira Island, Mele, Pango, Erakor and Eratap were hemmed in by the Colardeau, Russet, Ohlen, SIP and other plantations and their populations were growing quickly. Of these villages it was probably Ifira that felt the most constricted by European settlement. On Fila Island there was, moreover, a strong feeling, manifest increasingly during the 1960s and 1970s, that a much greater area of land situated between the Blacksands and La Colle Rivers, had been appropriated for European-owned plantations (Frouin, Bladinières) than was acknowledged to have been sold in 1872 to a Britisher named William Bassett. It was hardly surprising, therefore, that Dr. John Kalsakau, a brother of Chief Graham Kalsakau of Fila Island, was the leading New Hebridean spokesman on land in AdCo.

For most of the first two decades after the 1939–45 War, there was not very much new land development by Europeans. This relative stability in the extent of effective European land occupation began to change in the early 1960s, however, with the growth of cattle farming. Until this period, cattle had been regarded mainly as an adjunct to coconut planting, by keeping the grass short under the palms and providing meat for plantation labour, with some beef being sold to urban butchers. When some French landowners began extensive clearings of hitherto undeveloped land in south-east Santo, there was a New Hebridean reaction to this new phenomenon in the form of the Nagriamel movement. In the first 'Act of Dark Bush', drawn up in 1964 by joint leaders Mr. Jimmy Stevens and Chief Buluk, Nagriamel declared its objection to further European land development beyond existing plantations into the 'dark bush'.[9]

It was against this background of an apparent renewal of European land development on Santo, and to a lesser extent on Efate, that two major debates on this subject initiated by New Hebridean members, took place in AdCo in 1965 and 1967. Kalsakau was an articulate and eloquent exponent of Melanesian fears and resentments over land. He explained that in some cases, they knew land occupied by Europeans had not been properly bought. He pressed for the establishment of a land commission, which would investigate such cases. Kalsakau's line was moderate. Where investigation by the Commission showed a European title to have been based on a defective claim, it would be possible, excepting instances of actual Melanesian land shortage, for the European concerned to remain in occupation, after paying compensation to the villagers. Kalsakau was at pains to assure the Council that he was not arguing for an upheaval over land, as this would be bad for the New Hebrides. However, before there was further land development, based on title awarded by the Joint Court, it should be ascertained whether this would create local shortages for New Hebrideans.

Understandably enough, since the great majority of alienated land was in French ownership, the FR was opposed to the proposed land commission, since it feared that to go behind the decisions of the Joint Court, which the Protocol decreed to be final, would jeopardise the whole basis of non-native land ownership.

---

9   For further information on Nagriamel see J. Beasant, 1984, *The Santo Rebellion: an Imperial Reckoning*, Honolulu: Hawaii University Press; P. Bernard, 1983, I, Paris: Université Paris-X-Nanterre; B. Hours, 1974, *Un mouvement politico-religieux néo-hébridais: le Nagriamel, Cahiers ORSTOM* 11(3–4): 227–42; Hours, 1976, 'Leadership et cargo cult: l'irrésistible ascension de J.T.P.S. Moïse,' *Journal de la Société des Océanistes* 32(2): 207–31; W.F.S. Miles, 1998, *Bridging Mental Boundaries in a Postcolonial Microcosm: Identity and Development in Vanuatu*, Honolulu: University of Hawai'i Press; R. Shears, 1980, *The Coconut War: The Crisis on Espiritu Santo*, Sydney and Melbourne: Cassell Australia Limited; J.M. Stevens, 1995, 'The Nagriamel movement,' in *Melanesian Politics:* Stael Blong *Vanuatu*, ed. Howard Van Trease, Christchurch: Macmillan Brown Centre for Pacific Studies, University of Canterbury and Suva: Institute of Pacific Studies, University of South Pacific, pp. 227–34; A. Stuart, 2001, *Of Cargoes, Colonies and Kings: Diplomatic Administrative Service from Africa to the Pacific*, London and New York: The Radcliffe Press, pp. 129– 223; M. Tabani, 2008, 'The political history of the Nagriamel movement,' *Oceania* 78: 332–57.

Nevertheless, the BR was sympathetic to the idea of a commission, on the grounds that Europeans would benefit from the enhanced stability in a land tenure that would result from a fair settlement of land disputes between New Hebrideans and the holders of registered title. The land commission proposal was, however, left in limbo, although an *ad hoc* commission comprising both officials and some AdCo members did investigate a land dispute between two British title-holders and Melanesian villages at Bonkovia on Epi (1966). The investigation resulted in a compromise settlement of the dispute.

Disputes between New Hebrideans and Europeans over land became more frequent in the 1970s, especially when Europeans attempted to extend development on to land for which they held title but which had hitherto remained under bush. When these disputes occurred the District Agents did their best to bring about a settlement, but in most cases the Residencies also became involved. On a number of occasions I found myself discussing possible solutions with Fabre, my colleague at the FR, with whom I enjoyed an excellent working relationship over many years. In some of the more serious cases the dispute could only be ended, and possible breaches of public order avoided, by the European titleholder giving up part of his undeveloped land to the New Hebrideans who claimed custom ownership of it.

In the mid- to late-1970s, the RCs found it was necessary to send joint police detachments to deter villagers from taking possession of developed land owned by Europeans, although this type of dispute was exceptional. Land remained a political issue, but one that was not finally settled until independence, when non-indigenous freehold, based on titles awarded by the Joint Court, was abolished and all land was deemed to have reverted to New Hebridean customary ownership.

Nagriamel movement

As mentioned above, the Nagriamel movement was formed to resist the extension of European clearing of bush land for the purpose of grazing cattle. With its base at Vanafo, about twelve miles (19.3 kilometres) from Luganville, situated on land nominally owned by the SFNH, and where people from both the Santo bush and from outside Santo, especially Ambrym and Pentecost, had formed a community, the movement continued to oppose European land development in the 'dark bush' for the rest of the decade. In 1967, its joint leaders, Stevens and Buluk, together with a number of Ambrymese were prosecuted in the Court of First Instance for trespass and the removal of survey markers on land being purchased by William Ezra, (a Solomon Islander married to a New Hebridean) from a French settler named Allegre. Stevens and Buluk were sentenced to several months' imprisonment, and the Ambrymese men to lesser terms. Being anxious that Stevens and Buluk should not be seen as martyrs for trying to protect the 'dark bush' from further European encroachment, the BR procured a reduction in their sentences. As Stevens enjoyed the local status of British Protected Person, he served his sentence of four months in the British prison in Port Vila. I took advantage of his being there to talk to him on two or three occasions in my office, as I wanted to find out what sort of person he was, and to obtain some understanding of Nagriamel. On one of these occasions, I invited my FR counterpart, Jacques Fabre, to talk to Stevens, knowing as I did that Jimmy and his movement were considered by the FR to pose a great threat to French land interests on Santo and elsewhere. I found Stevens likeable and plausible, and possessing a degree of charisma, which explained the influence he had obtained over Santo bush people, and other New Hebrideans. I also came to the conclusion that he was genuine in wanting to protect bush land on Santo from further European expansion, whilst I suspected that he was also motivated by a degree of self-seeking. His later behaviour showed this suspicion to have been amply justified.

In the late 1960s and into the early 1970s, Nagriamel continued to agitate about land and in 1971 Jimmy Stevens even wrote to the United Nations, complaining that Nagriamel members had been chased off SFNH land on Malo Island by men with guns and a 'great big buggery dog!' The movement's influence was extended to some of the northern islands (Malekula, Ambae, Epi) and especially in places where there were existing grievances over land occupied or claimed by non-natives. However, the nature of the Nagriamel movement began to change in the early 1970s, as Stevens came under the influence of American land speculators, such as Harold Eugene Peacock and libertarian advocates, especially Michael Oliver and the Phoenix Foundation. By the mid-1970s, moreover, Stevens, once the bogey man of the FR and French settlers, had become their political ally.

Although I do not recall ever having discussed this subject with my French colleagues, I have always assumed the change in the FR's policy regarding Nagriamel to have resulted from it having come to realise, by the early 1970s, that it would be possible to do business with Stevens. André Leconte's dealings with Nagriamel over land (see below) would not have gone unnoticed by our colleagues. The adoption by the FR of a policy of returning undeveloped French State land to Melanesian ownership (especially on Malekula and Santo) may have influenced Stevens' attitude towards the FR. Stevens was, moreover, venal and one cannot exclude the possibility that he envisaged obtaining financial gain by co-operating with the FR either directly via the French District Agency in Luganville, or indirectly through the alliance with Mouvement pour L'Autonomie des Nouvelles-Hébride (MANH). Be this as it may, the FR's enlightened decision to help the Nagriamel community at Vanafo by providing a dispensary and either a school, or a water supply scheme, or both, must have shown the movement's leadership the material advantages of getting on side with the French, apart from their hostility to the NP.

Before leaving, for the time being, the subject of land, I must not omit to mention the wave of land speculation that began in or about 1967, with the arrival on the scene of Harold Eugene Peacock, who had previously been based in Hawai'i. Peacock came to the New Hebrides at a time when a number of French landowners were feeling some uncertainty about the political and economic future of the territory, and were by no means averse to selling land to Peacock. By 1970, or possibly earlier, he had acquired six properties, mainly on Santo, including one near Hog Harbour, purchased from a M. Graziani. Peacock's long-term intention was the subdivision of these properties into small plots, which he hoped to sell to Americans, and especially people who wanted a free and easy life style, with little taxation. His advertisements in Honolulu and elsewhere described his subdivisions, and their as yet non-existent amenities, in glowing and misleading terms.

The BR, in particular, viewed Peacock's subdivision schemes with considerable misgivings. We feared that the settlement on Santo of several hundred, possibly more than a thousand, new American and other immigrants, would cause an adverse reaction amongst New Hebrideans, who were, as we have seen, already showing their concern regarding land alienation. We also thought that these new immigrants would expect, or even demand, public services which did not exist and which the Condominium could not afford to provide. In 1970 and 1971, therefore, we began to urge on the FR (Robert Langlois was then FRC) the need for legislation to enable the Joint Administration to control the subdivision of land. Our colleagues, however, viewed the matter with less concern, partly because they realised that some French landowners welcomed the unexpected, and very agreeable, opportunity of selling advantageously land which they might not have been able to develop.

When, after much delay, a joint regulation for the control of subdivisions was finally issued in 1971 it was made retrospective in order to make its provisions applicable to the subdivisions which Mr Peacock was in the process of creating. This joint regulation (Joint Regulation No.15 of 1971) contained a clause to the effect that if an application to the Joint Administration for the approval of a subdivision had not been either approved or rejected within six months, it was deemed to have been approved. After Peacock had submitted applications for his subdivisions, month after month went by and it seemed increasingly likely that the FR was playing for time in order that the applications, which the BR opposed, would go through by default when the six months had elapsed. It took a special visit to Port Vila by Inspecteur-Général Jean-Jacques Robert (who was to be the last FRC, 1978–80) to bring the FR around to the British point of view, and the consequent rejection of the Peacock subdivisions. Infuriated by this rebuff to his subdivision projects, Peacock resorted to legal action. Although he had opted for the French legal system as an individual,[10] he had registered his company under British Company legislation. Either because of these circumstances, or because he was well aware that it was the BR that had defeated his projects, he instituted a law-suit against the BRC, Colin Allan, and the Assistant BRC, Mike Townsend, alleging that the giving of retrospective effect to the Joint Subdivision Regulation so as to reject his applications was an abuse of power, being both unconstitutional and inequitable.

That the BR had been justified in its apprehension of an adverse New Hebridean reaction to the arrival in the group of large numbers of purchasers of plots of Peacock's projected subdivisions was shown to be valid in 1971. In the middle of that year, a demonstration in Port Vila to support the Joint Subdivision Regulation was organised by the newly-formed NP. I was absent on leave in Britain at the time, but it is my understanding that some leading New Hebrideans had become aware of mounting European settler opposition to the RCs' policy of controlling subdivisions. This demonstration was the first significant public action undertaken by the NP, which had originated, early in 1971, with a group of educated New Hebrideans, including Donald Kalpokas and Peter Taurakoto, who formed the New Hebrides Cultural Association. These two persons were both BR Assistant Education Officers. Thus began the ever-increasing involvement with the NP (as the Cultural Association became) of New Hebrideans employed by the BR.

British and French relations in the movement towards independence

Because a large number of the confidential monthly reports sent by the FR to the French Government in Paris were carelessly left in boxes outside the French Offices, where they were discovered on 31 July 1980, it is known what the views of successive FRCs on Condominium matters were from 1966 until 1978. I also know how I was regarded by my French colleagues during at least part of that period. In his report for December 1966, M. Jacques Mouradian (FRC 1964–69) said that the AdCo session for that month had been a quiet one, because Woodward, then on leave, had not been around to do any stirring! I was, in fact never guilty of inciting AdCo members to raise awkward

---

10 Expatriates, who were nationals of neither Britain nor France, were required by the Protocol to opt within one month of arriving in the New Hebrides for either the British or French legal systems. They then became what was known as either British or French *ressortissants* and, if subsequently charged with a criminal offence, or sued under civil law, their cases fell to be treated under the legal system for which they had opted.

questions. Again, the FRC's report for May 1970, referred to me as *'l'expert le plus chevronné de la Résidence Britannique en demagogie appliquée'* (the BR's most experienced and hard-working expert in demagoguery)! This remark, equally unmerited, was made in connection with my accompanying Mr. George Kalkoa as his adviser to the Waigani Seminar (at Port Moresby) on the Politics of Melanesia. Much more important, however, was the inclusion, in the Report for September or October 1969, the last one sent by Mouradian, of his recommendations as to future French policy in the New Hebrides.

Mouradian contended that France could protect her long-term interests in the New Hebrides beyond independence by strengthening and increasing its influence among the New Hebridean population. To achieve this objective France should get as many Melanesian children as possible into French education. Also, since medical services and the co-operative's support services were important to the New Hebrideans, these services, like education, should remain under French control, as an additional means of maintaining and increasing French influence. In contrast, the British, had few national interests in the New Hebrides, and were anxious to divest themselves of their responsibilities in the Condominium. As France needed time to achieve its objectives, it would be necessary to resist British pressure for rapid constitutional advance, and for the unification of the nationally-operated public services.

It was, indeed, British policy to work for the unification of public services provided separately by the two Condominium partners. In pursuance of this objective, there had been discussions in the mid-1960s between the British and French Chief Medical Officers, initiated on our side, about the replacement of the existing hospitals in Port Vila,[11] which were old and inadequate, by a single jointly-operated new hospital. The French attitude had been sufficiently encouraging for the BR to believe that a joint hospital was a real possibility, so that planning for a new British Government hospital to replace Paton Memorial Hospital had been suspended for a year or more. When it finally became clear that France had, in fact, no intention of being involved in a joint hospital, there was a feeling in the BR that we had been misled, with the result that the construction of the much-needed new British Hospital had been needlessly delayed (it was not finally commissioned until mid-1975). The unification of national services did not take place until after my departure from the New Hebrides, although by that time (March 1978), independence was clearly not far off, and partial self-government had been instituted.

---

11 The older, the European, part of the French Hospital, in which I was very well looked after for three weeks in 1953, dated from 1911, and Paton Memorial Hospital on Iririki, built by the Presbyterian Mission, also dated from 1911. Both hospitals had given great and devoted service to the people of Port Vila and beyond. For me, and many others, the French hospital will always be associated with that wonderful lady, Soeur Marie-Adrien, who was its Matron for so many years, known affectionately as Soeur Marie Pique-fesse!

AdCo, parties and 'people power'

By 1969 the second AdCo had lasted for five years and it was obviously time for a change. Although there had been two meetings at Ministerial level about the Condominium in the mid-1960s, they had not resulted in any alteration in the French Government's position regarding constitutional advance, and it is to be presumed that Mouradian's recommendations had fallen on receptive ears in Paris. The BR therefore had no choice but to continue with the AdCo, which had already been in existence for eleven years. The two Residencies agreed, however, that the number of private, or unofficial, members should be increased from twenty to twenty-four, and that there should be eight instead of four New Hebridean members indirectly elected by local council members. There would be a small, but not insignificant departure from the principle of absolute parity of representation between New Hebridean and non-natives. While the number of New Hebridean (indirectly) elected members was increased from four to eight, that of non-native members chosen by the Chamber of Commerce Electoral College would only rise from four to six.

Although there had been some increase in the number of Local Councils representing New Hebrideans since 1964, there were still several islands or parts of islands, not covered by councils. Now that the number of indirectly elected AdCo members was to be doubled to eight, it would have been unfair to a significant proportion of the New Hebridean population for all of these members to be chosen exclusively by the Local Councils. In consultation with the District Agents, therefore, it was decided that the electoral colleges for each of the four Districts would, in addition to Local Council members, also include representatives of non-Council villagers. When suggesting this arrangement to my French colleague I was by no means sure how it would work in practice, but in the event, our ever-resourceful District Agents were able to organise the representation for the non-Council areas on the electoral colleges to the apparent satisfaction of all concerned.

Because of the distance in time, I cannot, unfortunately recall much about the changes in membership between the 1964 to 1969 AdCo, and its successor. I remember that George Kalkoa (later Ati George Sokomanu) was elected by the Central District No. 1 (CD1) Electoral College, and (to my regret) Dr. John Kalsakau ceased to be a member. Fr. Gérard Leymang was one of the six nominated New Hebridean members. On the European side, M. Philippe Delacroix, a Port Vila businessman, became a member, and the leader of the Anglican Church in the New Hebrides, Archdeacon Derek Rawcliffe, replaced Pastor Bob Murray. The new AdCo was much less docile than its predecessors, and when it was convened for the 1971–72 (or 1973) end of year budget session, the members refused to begin examining the Condominium Estimates until they had been granted an immediate adjournment for a few days, so that they could study and discuss them. The estimates had been given to them only after their arrival in Port Vila. There was more pressure from members on all sides of the Council, and especially from the British and New Hebrideans, for the replacement of AdCo by a legislative body. There was also demand for land reform, in which George Kalkoa was prominent.

AdCo members, and other people agitating for more constitutional advance, especially the recently-formed NP, received a cold douche when a high-ranking French Minister, M. Pierre Mesmer, visited the New Hebrides in May 1972. In a speech delivered to a large audience at the reception in his honour at the FR, he squarely stated that the time was not ripe for constitutional advance at central government level. Instead, the people of the New Hebrides should prepare themselves for that by learning how to run their own affairs through experience in local government. I was present when Mesmer made this oration, and I immediately appreciated its significance. We would have to wait for a few more years before the Condominium could progress beyond the AdCo stage.

The NP, however, was in no mood to conform patiently with Mesmer's views. By 1973, its President, the young Anglican priest, Fr. Walter Lini, was already calling for independence to be brought about by 1977, and the party's membership, which was overwhelmingly composed of anglophone Melanesians, and adherents of the Presbyterian and Anglican churches, was growing rapidly. By the end of that year, moreover, the NP had shown its teeth in no uncertain manner.

On 27 December 1973 the NP, which the British Police had known to be planning a demonstration at least two or three days ahead, swarmed into the grounds of the FR Secretariat to demand the immediate release from the French prison in Santo of two brothers of the prominent Rarua family of Tongoa, who were held on remand accused of assaulting a *milicien* (a Melanesian constable in the French Police Force). This was a controversial case, and it had been agreed at Residency level that it should be tried by the Joint Court, and not the Native Court, which would otherwise have had jurisdiction. In the meantime, the Acting FRC, Jacques Fabre, had agreed with us that the two accused should be released, pending the trial. Unfortunately, and although (knowing the NP demonstration was likely) I had called on Fabre at home on Sunday 26 December to urge the immediate release of the two men: this was not ordered in time. The result was that Fabre had to agree, from the veranda of the French Office, to telephone Santo to obtain the brothers' release from gaol, under pressure of a shouting mob of New Hebrideans. I had accompanied the Assistant BRC, Mike Townsend, to the scene, in order to talk to the NP leaders, and to try and ensure things did not get out of hand. I shall always remember the sight of the personnel of the FR, looking understandably somewhat apprehensive, clustered along the veranda railings. The future President of Vanuatu, Kalkot Matas Kele-

Kele (2004–2009), then very much a young political firebrand, appeared to be orchestrating the demonstration and I recall trying to calm him down. I stayed around talking to demonstrators, who were not really in a dangerous mood, until they began to disperse. Detachments of both the British and French Police Forces had tried to prevent the demonstration occupying the Secretariat garden but had been ignored. It was, I suppose one could say, the first show of people power in the New Hebrides. More was to follow.

Up to this point, the NP had no rivals on the political scene, although I recall Philippe Delacroix, ex-parachutist and future hard-line Santo secessionist, made a well-meant, but short-lived, first attempt to form a moderate progressive party, which he named, Union des Populations des Nouvelles-Hébrides (UPNH). Such support as UPNH had was among francophone New Hebrideans, and I remember one of them coming to talk to me about it. I was friendly with Delacroix, as we were both members of the Board of Management of the Port Vila Cultural Centre.

Early in January 1974, and probably in reaction to the NP's 27 December demonstration, which arose from a matter concerning Santo, the Mouvement pour L'Autonomie des Nouvelles-Hébrides (MANH) was formed in Luganville.[12] This movement had as its core membership the French population of Santo. There were also some francophone New Hebridean adherents, including the late Aimé Maleré of North Malekula. I seem to remember that the name of the movement was felt to be too radical, and was soon changed to, Mouvement Autonomiste des Nouvelles-Hébrides, but it didn't really matter, as the party was invariably known as MANH. I do not recall that it had any particular policy, other than that of opposition to the NP, and the traditional Santo dislike of Port Vila. Despite the word *autonomie* or *autonomiste* in its title, MANH was not in favour of early independence. Jimmy Stevens' Nagriamel shared MANH's antipathy towards the NP, and the two movements were to become closely linked, being usually referred to as MANH-Nagriamel.

It is probably true to say that UCNH, which was set up in March or April 1974, also owed much to a movement of reaction against the NP, aggravated by the latter's demonstration at the FR. UCNH was, despite its name, essentially the party of the French people living in Port Vila and in the southern New Hebrides, together with francophone New Hebrideans. Whilst declaring itself favourable to constitutional advance, UCNH opposed the early independence demanded by

---

12 For further information on the origins of MANH see Kalkot Matas Kele-Kele, 1977, 'The emergence of political parties,' in *New Hebrides: Road to Independence*, ed. Chris Plant, Suva: Institute of Pacific Studies, University of South Pacific, pp. 17–34, pp. 30–32. Howard Van Trease, 1995, 'Colonial origins of Vanuatu politics,' in *Melanesian Politics: Stael Blong Vanuatu*, ed. Howard Van Trease, Christchurch: Macmillan Brown Centre for Pacific Studies, University of Canterbury and Suva: Institute of Pacific Studies, University of South Pacific, pp. 3–58, pp. 26–27.

the NP. Its francophone Melanesian members, who were mainly Catholic, feared that a NP Government could threaten French education, and the employment of francophones. Among its principal leaders were the popular Rémy Delaveuve, a keen footballer, Guy Prévot, and Jean-Marie Leyhe, an AdCo member. Leymang and Vincent Boulekone also became prominent members of UCNH.

In July 1974 the NP staged another demonstration in Port Vila, and briefly occupied the Condominium Office building. This was in protest about a New Hebridean being killed on the Mele road by a European, notorious for fast driving.

British and French dialogues on the future

During 1973 and 1974 we were hearing from the Foreign Office in London that there was soon to be an Anglo-French Ministerial meeting to discuss the future of the New Hebrides, but this meeting did not, in fact, take place until November 1974. Early in that year the Gaullist President of France, M. George Pompidou, died and had been replaced by the more liberal Valery Giscard d'Estaing. I have always thought that it was this change at the top which brought about a reversal of the previous French Government policy of resistance to constitutional advance in the New Hebrides. However, the coming into being at the beginning of 1974 of two francophone political parties, both of which wanted greater popular participation in the running of the Condominium, (even if they were opposed to independence) may also have had a bearing on the new willingness of the French Government to consider some degree of movement towards self-government.

When the November 1974 date for the long-awaited Anglo-French Ministerial meeting had been fixed, the British and French Residencies in the New Hebrides were given only a comparatively short time to prepare joint proposals for consideration by Ministers. The two RCs, Mr. R.W.H. (later Sir Roger) du Boulay and M. M.R. Langlois, were to take these proposals with them to London, where they would attend the meeting.

Soon after the date of the Ministerial meeting was announced du Boulay asked me to accompany him to the FR, as he had arranged to discuss with Langlois the preparations for the London talks. Somewhat to my surprise, the Chancelier, Jacques Fabre, was not present. It had obviously been made known to the FR that the French Government was at last ready to contemplate a significant further stage of constitutional advance, since Langlois very quickly evoked the prospect of elections being held in the New Hebrides. At this point, I must mention, since it will make clearer what follows, that by this time (October 1974), the NP had a high profile, because of its demands for early independence, and the two large demonstrations that it had held in Port Vila in December

1973 and July 1974. The NP had thus become something of a bogey for the French population of the Condominium, and its policies were viewed with some apprehension by francophone New Hebrideans.

The FRC expressed anxiety as to the likely reaction of the French community, perhaps some kind of backlash, in the event of the NP obtaining a large majority in future elections. He wondered whether the chances of such an outcome could be lessened by the *découpage* (fixing the boundaries) of electoral constituencies. Du Boulay lent forward, 'Ah,' he said, 'you mean gerrymandering.' It was with difficulty that I stopped myself from laughing at the frankness of this remark, as it was perfectly obvious to me that Langlois had meant precisely that, although he had put the matter more delicately. The term gerrymandering, with its connotations of fixing electoral boundaries in Northern Ireland to prevent the fair representation of Roman Catholics in that troubled province, is sometimes used in France, but if Langlois knew its pejorative nature, he showed no sign of taking offence at his colleague's use of it.

For me, this discussion, at which I was so glad to have been present, was most instructive. I shared the FRC's apprehension at the possibility of the NP obtaining a big majority of the seats in the forthcoming elections, because I knew that this majority could be even greater than its potential electoral support in the New Hebridean population would justify, especially if we failed to give very careful consideration to the arrangement of electoral constituencies, and the voting system. This was because the New Hebrideans opposed to the NP, although forming a significant minority (at least one third of the overall indigenous population), did not constitute a majority in any of the major islands, with the possible exception of Tanna. I realised, therefore, that anything resembling the British electoral system, with its single-seat constituencies, and first past the post voting system, would have to be avoided.

Designing an electoral system for the New Hebrides

If I dwell somewhat at length on this subject, I must ask the reader's indulgence, because it is true to say that the electoral system still in use in Vanuatu today owes its origin to that meeting between Messrs du Boulday, Langlois and me at the FR in October 1974, and to the inspiration that I derived from it.

Because Jacques Fabre had not been present at the discussion referred to above, it was, I suppose, normal that I should take the initiative in preparing proposals for the approval of the two RCs, and submission to the Ministers at the London meeting. I had, moreover, much more time than had Fabre to devote to the matter.

As Secretary for Political Affairs at the BR, my primary function was to deal with constitutional advance, and I had little else, at that time, to distract my attention from this subject. In his position as Chancelier at the FR (as No.2 to the FRC) Fabre had much less time to give to political matters, as—with the probable exception of finance—just about everything with which the FR was concerned passed over his desk. In these circumstances, I think he was content for me to do the initial spade work, as I found subsequently that he had not prepared proposals on his own account. It was the unwritten convention between the Residencies, and the most practical and sensible way of working the Condominium system of administration, for one Residency to work on the details of a given project and then to submit proposals for the agreement of the other Residency, rather than for both to be working on a given matter simultaneously, and in detail. Thus, when the decision in principle had been taken by the two Governments that municipal authorities should be set up in Port Vila and Santo, we in the BR were content to let the French prepare a project based on French local government practice, although I made a point, in 1971, of spending several days in a typical small 'commune' in France to see for myself how the French system worked.

When considering what kind of electoral system would be appropriate for the inauguration of democracy in the New Hebrides, my primary concern was the need to ensure that it should be fair to each of the main political, or quasi-political groups. It seemed to me that the key to the problem was *découpage*, the word mentioned by Langlois, concerning the arrangement of constituencies. Although du Boulay had interpreted *découpage* as gerrymandering, this may well not have been Langlois' intention, and I felt reasonably confident that our purpose could be achieved in an objective way. We had not much time to prepare proposals for the London conference.

To ensure reasonably balanced representation in the future legislative body of the main political interests, something akin to proportional representation (PR) would be needed. However, no information about PR systems was available to me, and, in any case, I knew that such systems usually involved complicated voting arrangements, which would not be suitable for the New Hebrides, where nearly everybody would be voting for the first time, and where, moreover, many voters would be illiterate. It was essential, therefore, that our electoral system should be fairly simple, so that as many people as possible could cast valid votes.

The main problem was posed by the rural areas of the Group, with their population spread over many islands, some large and some small. A separate, and different, electoral system would be needed for the two towns of Port Vila and Luganville, in which the populations were more concentrated. I quickly came to the conclusion that the division of the New Hebrides, Banks and Torres into single-seat constituencies would result in the NP obtaining more representatives in the future legislature than its strength could justify. This was because the NP, which drew its support from the numerous members of the Presbyterian and Anglican Churches, was in the majority in so many islands, whereas its opponents were scattered around the islands, although constituting about a third of the Melanesian population. They were the adherents of the Catholic and French Protestant Churches, the followers of the John Frum and Nagriamel movements, together with pagan communities, such as the Big and Small Nambas on Malekula, and 'custom' people on Pentecost, Ambrym, Malo and Tanna. As for the minority anglophone Protestant Churches or 'sects', at that time the Church of Christ, the Apostolic Church (based only on Ambae) and the Seventh-day Adventists, I think their political allegiance was divided. Many, perhaps most, Church of Christ members opposed the NP because of their Church's association with Jimmy Stevens and Nagriamel. I do not know whether the Seventh-day Adventists, who were present in small communities on Santo, Aore, Ambae, Tanna and in the Shepherd Islands, were NP supporters or not.

The division of each of the largest or most populous islands of Espiritu Santo, Malekula and Tanna into two or three constituencies would have been difficult without the Joint Administration being suspected of gerrymandering for the purpose of favouring the electoral chances of one or other of the political groups. Therefore, I dismissed at the outset of my planning any ideas of such divisions. Instead, I chose the alternative of making these islands multi-seat constituencies, with each returning three representatives.

In opting for multi-seat constituencies, I also had in mind the existence on each of these three islands of a substantial political minority, which ought to be represented in the legislature. Thus, the three-seat Santo constituency (which would include Malo, Aore and the nearby small islands along its coasts) could be expected to have a majority of NP supporters, because so many Presbyterians lived in it. In comparison, the adherents of Nagriamel and Tabwemasama constituted a significant political minority opposing the NP, and should certainly be represented. Likewise the three-seat constituency of Malekula and nearby small islands, although having a majority of Presbyterians, who would vote for the NP, also had a significant anti-NP minority of Catholics, Nagriamel adherents and Charlemagne Protestants, who had to be represented. On Tanna, however, supporters and opponents of the NP were more evenly divided. Whilst the Presbyterians could be expected to vote for the NP, the adherents of John Frum and people in 'custom' villages would not, and they might form the majority of the island.

The problem confronting us was not only one of creating objectively valid electoral constituencies for the whole of the New Hebrides, Banks and Torres Islands, but also one of devising a system of voting for a rural population of which many members were illiterate. It was most important that it should be simple, so as to minimise the number of wasted, unfulfilled votes.

I discussed this matter with Fabre. We agreed that, at least where the rural voters were concerned, people should not have to be able to read candidates' names on ballot-papers, and be required to indicate their choice by marking the papers, for example, by putting a cross against the chosen name. Jacques told me that, in some French territories (I think New Caledonia was mentioned) voters were given, upon entering the polling station, ballot-papers for each of the candidates. These not only bore the candidate's name, but also the electoral symbol of his party, and were in different colours, according to the candidate's party. The voter had to take the ballot-papers of all the candidates into the polling booth, where he or she would pick out the one of his or her choice, and then deposit it in the ballot-box in an envelope, leaving the other papers in the polling booth. I immediately recognised the value of this system.

There are a number of different systems of proportional representation in use around the world, but none of them would have been suited to our requirements. What I sought to achieve was an electoral system which would give roughly proportional results, by ensuring as far as reasonably possible, that the various political parties were represented.

As the date of the election approached, and I gave further thought to the mechanics of voting, I foresaw a difficulty that would confront illiterate voters in the multi-seat constituencies. They would be given a ballot paper for each of the candidates put up by the various parties contesting the constituency. It was very important, indeed vital, that every voter, illiterate as well as literate, should be able to distinguish between the ballot papers of the candidates of his chosen party, as he would have been told by that party's election organisers which candidate to cast his ballot for. It happened that Kalkot Matas Kele-Kele came into my office one day when I was thinking about these matters (I rarely thought about much else), or perhaps I had asked him to drop by. Kalkot, who had begun a law course a year or so earlier at the University of Papua New Guinea, Port Moresby, had obtained permission to take a year out, in order to organise the NP's election campaign. I explained the voting system to him, and in the course of doing so, mentioned the problem of illiterate voters. It is possible that it only occurred to me then, as I talked to him—I am not sure now. Be that as it may, Kalkot said to me, 'What about putting photographs on the ballot papers?' I saw at once that this was the answer, and wondered why I hadn't thought of it myself.

When I discussed the use of candidates' photos on ballot papers with my colleague at the FR, I did not tell him that the idea had come from Kalkot. This was not because I wished to claim the credit for someone else's idea, but because of the very strong anti-NP feeling in the FR. This made me afraid that the photo idea might be rejected, if its origin was known. In fact, the value of photographs was immediately appreciated by the FR, despite the additional expense and organisational work that would be involved.

An essential element of the proposal that I prepared for the agreement of the FR was the creation of multi-member constituencies, that is, with either two or three seats in the legislature, for each of those areas of the Condominium where there were substantial numbers of people supporting the NP and opposing it. In other areas, where the people were all of one political persuasion, because they all, or virtually all, belonged to one religious denomination, there would be single-member constituencies. The three-member ones would be Santo (excluding Luganville), Malekula and Tanna and the two-member ones would be Ambae-Maevo, Pentecost and Ambrym. The single-member constituencies would be Banks and Torres, Epi-Paama and Tongoa-Shepherd Islands, Efate (excluding Port Vila) and nearby small islands, and finally Southern District Outer Islands (Erromango, Aneytium, Futuna and Aniwa). Almost all of the populations of these last five constituencies belonged to the Presbyterian and Anglican Churches from which the NP derived nearly all its support.

The second essential element was the principle of only one vote to be cast by each elector. Allied with this was the principle that illiteracy would not prevent anyone from casting a valid vote.

To help the reader understand my proposed electoral system, and how I hoped to achieve the approximate proportional representation of the political parties, I shall take Malekula as an example. Together with its numerous nearby islands, such as the Maskelynes, Vao and Atchin, Malekula was to be a three-member constituency. The majority of its population was Presbyterian, and could be expected to support the NP, but there was a substantial minority which would not. This minority was composed of the Catholics of the Lamap-Port Sandwich area, and those inhabiting the islands of Vao, Wala and Rano, together with the Charlemagne Protestant community of North-East Malekula, and some Nagriamel villagers. I thought that these various groups probably amounted to about one-third of the population of the constituency. There were Seventh-day Adventists (SDAs) on Atchin Island, and at Tenmaru, N.W. Malekula, but I did not know where their political sympathies lay.

There were enough NP supporters in the constituency to return two NP members to the Assembly, and enough people opposed to the NP to elect the third member. If things turned out like that, well and good, and there would be proportional representation of this constituency. Such a desirable result could not, however, be counted on. Each of the political parties contesting Malekula had the choice of putting up one, two or three candidates. If, as was likely, the NP decided to field three, its election organisers would be well advised to make sure, as far as they could by canvassing the party's supporters, that the latter did not all vote for one particularly well-known, or popular person. If they were not to do that, the NP could end up winning only one of the three seats, instead of the two, which its numerical strength made attainable. Conversely, their opponents, if unwise enough to present three candidates, could let the NP win all three seats, especially if their limited voting strength was to be spread more or less evenly over their candidates. If that happened, each of their three candidates might get fewer votes than any one of the NP's. To prevent either of these equally undesirable outcomes, voters in every part of the large Malekula constituency would need to observe strict discipline in obeying the instructions of their party's officials as to which of its candidates to vote for.

The twin dangers of the bunching of votes on only one candidate out of two or three, and that of the votes of the minority party being thinly spread over too many candidates, were inherent in this proposed electoral system. They would, therefore, confront party organisers in each of the two- and three-member constituencies. If my colleague, Jacques Fabre, accepted my proposals, despite these dangers, it was presumably because he realised that they offered the best chance of the political minorities opposed to the NP being fairly represented, and that any alternative system would unduly favour the majority NP. It seems that our respective RCs were content with what we had agreed upon. My boss, Mr. du Boulay, never questioned me about them. I later inferred from one of his file minutes that he thought the FR had originated them, and I was quite content to let him continue in this assumption. The important thing was that both Ministers and our local politicians should regard the electoral arrangements as being equally favoured by each Residency. If it had come to the ears of UCNH, or MANH-Nagriamel that I was the author of them, they would immediately have suspected the system was designed to ensure the victory of the NP. In fact, of course, it was intended to ensure, if only they understood the opportunities for them that it offered, that these minority groups got a fair crack of the electoral whip.

In the event, when the election for the first Representative Assembly (RA) was held on 1 November 1975, the electoral system that I have tried to describe above yielded the kind of result that I had hoped for. I do not, however, wish to anticipate matters by writing in any detail about that election at this stage. For the present, it will suffice to say that the two main political parties, the NP and the Modérés (Moderates), as the FR was pleased to call the collection of parties and movements opposing the NP, obtained respectively the number of seats corresponding fairly closely to the percentages of votes cast for them. Something approximating to proportional representation was thus achieved, without the complexity of a formal PR system, with no NP landslide victory, and the Moderates winning at least one seat in every one of the two and three member constituencies.

I am conscious of having dwelt at considerable length on the electoral system for the RA, and I must hope that my readers have not been either too bored, or somewhat confused, by this rather arcane subject. I plead forgiveness on two grounds, however. The first is that the system continued to be used, not only for the 1979 parliamentary elections, but also for such elections beyond Independence, perhaps because it was found easier to keep what already existed than to devise a new system, a process which might have led to a good deal of controversy, since one or other of the political parties would probably have thought itself to be disadvantaged. The second is that I regard my work on constitutional advance, beginning with the introduction of indirect elections for AdCo in 1964, going on (in close co-operation with Jacques Fabre) to the planning of municipal government in the early 1970s, then culminating in the 1975 electoral system, as my most worthwhile achievements during my career at the BR.

London conference in 1974 and constitutional developments

At the London Conference in November 1974, at which the British Government was represented by Miss Joan Lestor, then a junior minister in the Foreign Office and the French by M. Olivier Stirn, then Secretary of State for Overseas Departments and Territories, the first major decisions concerning the future constitutional development of the New Hebrides were taken for more than twenty years.[13] These included the establishment of a Representative Assembly upon which would be conferred fairly wide legislative powers and the majority of the members of which were to be elected by universal suffrage. Ministers also decided that Municipal and Rural Community Councils, likewise to be based on universal suffrage, should be established in the New Hebrides. It was intended that the Rural Community Councils should progressively replace the Local

---

13　In this and in the three following paragraphs the narrative will begin to incorporate part – here paragraphs 7 to 10 – of the rather long history of constitutional advance, which I wrote in January–February 1978, and which was an official document, intended for circulation by the Foreign and Commonwealth Office to British diplomatic posts in countries likely to have an interest in the New Hebrides. It also went to the Governors of the remaining British dependent territories of the South Pacific. See Keith Woodward, 'Keith Woodward – Historical summary of constitutional advance in the New Hebrides, 1954-1977,' Canberra: Pacific Manuscripts Bureau, [2001], held State Library of New South Wales, Manuscripts, Oral History and Pictures, online: http://acms.sl.nsw.gov.au/item/itemDetailPaged.aspx?itemID=441498, accessed 21 July 2014.

Councils, which had been functioning in some islands—with varying degrees of success—for from ten to fifteen years, but which the FR had never regarded as satisfactory.

The RA was to include a certain number of members who would specifically represent economic interests. Following discussions between the British and French Residencies and further reference to the two Governments, the proposals for the composition of the Assembly which were submitted to the last session of AdCo in April 1975 provided for six members to be elected by the Chamber of Commerce Electoral College and for three members to be chosen by the combined governing Committees of the British and French supervised Co-operatives Associations. The six members to be chosen by the Chamber of Commerce Electorate would be non-New Hebridean, that is, persons of either British or French legal status, as were the Chamber of Commerce electors. Although the Chamber of Commerce Electoral College had been considerably expanded—to about six hundred persons—by 1975 (as a result of two new sections being added to the Chamber), this particular kind of representation was the direct descendent of the Chamber of Commerce representation in AdCo, which had already been severely criticised by AdCo members as early as 1969, when the then FRC, Mouradian, stated that he would not want to see this kind of representation in a successor body to AdCo. The three members of the Assembly chosen by the co-operatives' governing bodies were, of course, to be New Hebrideans since the membership of co-operative societies was exclusively indigenous.

Although the RA, as envisaged by Ministers at the London Conference, was not intended to include custom chiefs, the decision to do so was taken within two months, as a result of proposals made by leading New Hebrideans (not as a specifically political party idea) during the visit of Miss Lestor and M. Stirn to Port Vila in January 1975. AdCo at its final meeting in April that year approved the Residencies' proposal to include four chiefs in the RA to be elected—one for each District—by an Electoral College of Chiefs divided into four sections.

It is of minor historical interest to note that the Ministers agreed at the London Conference that two more New Hebridean members should be added to AdCo for the double purpose of giving New Hebrideans a majority, and of providing specific representation in the Council for the two major political parties, since one member was to be nominated by the NP and the other by UCNH. Thus, for the last two meetings of AdCo in December 1974 and April 1975, its total membership rose to thirty-two, including fourteen New Hebrideans and twelve European private members. In a lengthy document dated 13 January 1975 and submitted to the RCs immediately prior to the arrival of the two Ministers at Port Vila, the NP rigorously criticised the decisions taken at the London Conference, both because of their content and because no representatives of the New Hebridean people had taken part in the Conference. Some account was taken by the Residencies of the NP's criticisms of the composition proposed for the Assembly, since the number of rural seats was increased from seventeen to twenty and the number of members to represent Economic Interests was reduced from the original twelve to nine. As provided in the Exchange of Notes between the British and French Governments of 29 August 1975,[14] the RA was to be composed of forty-two members—twenty-nine to be elected by universal suffrage, nine to represent Economic Interests and four Chiefs. Whilst the twenty members who were to represent the rural areas would be elected by all communities voting on a common roll without distinction of race or legal status, a rather elaborate cross-voting system was instituted for the representation of the two towns, where the great majority of the non-New Hebridean population resided. The purpose of this system, as indeed of the representation of Economic Interests through the Chamber of Commerce Electorate, was to ensure that a minimum number of non-natives would be included in the Assembly, although it was fully accepted by the two Governments that there would be a substantial majority of New Hebrideans, since virtually all of the rural members could be expected to be indigenous. The representation of the two towns was prescribed as follows:

- Port Vila – two British, two French and two New Hebridean members
- Santo – one British, one French and one New Hebridean.

In the two towns, people in each community, British, French and New Hebridean, were obliged to vote for at least one candidate in each of the three legal categories, failing which their votes would not be valid.

The joint visit to the New Hebrides of Miss Joan Lestor and M. Olivier Stirn was a memorable occasion in the short history of the Condominium. Ministerial visits were rare events on both sides and I think I am safe in asserting that there had never before been a joint visit of British and French Ministers. I recall sitting next to Joan Lestor, a rather Junoesque, and quite attractive lady, on a social occasion at the BR on Iririki, and explaining to her some aspect or other of local politics. She listened politely, but I did not feel that the matter could have been of much interest to her, lacking as she probably was, relevant background knowledge. I also had a brief chat with Olivier Stirn. He did not ask me any questions, but proceeded, at some length, and with considerable enthusiasm, to expound to me the desirability of having television in the New Hebrides. Fortunately, he did not ask me what I thought about his idea, which bristled with practical difficulties, not least of which was the dispersal of the greater part of the population beyond the range of television transmitters in Port Vila and

---

14 The normal way of effecting amendments to the Protocol.

Luganville. I couldn't help wondering whether Stirn saw TV as a kind of sop to the masses, a means of distracting the New Hebridean population from political aspirations, and especially demands for independence.

The two Ministers held a joint meeting with Members of AdCo (and perhaps also political leaders but I am not sure now). They must have talked about the decisions taken at the London Conference, and no doubt invited questions and comments. It was at this meeting, which I attended (but only have a hazy memory of) that the suggestion was made that some chiefs should be included in the future RA. I cannot recall who made it, but it received general support, and probably appeared harmless to the two Ministers. The Moderates, and no doubt the FR, would have seen the inclusion of chiefs as another means of countering radical NP influence in the Assembly. It was not then foreseen that the choosing of the chiefs would be politicised. The question of independence did come up at the meeting with Ministers, and one of the NP AdCo Members—it may have been Iolu Abbil—expressed the opinion that it would, or should, come about by 1980. This proved to be an accurate prediction, or expression of hope.

It is still my opinion now, as it was in 1975, that the composition proposed for the first RA was fair and reasonable, given the circumstances of the time. It was devised to ensure that there would be a minimum of twelve non-native members, but these would be heavily outnumbered—nearly three times—by the New Hebrideans. The contribution of the European community to the economy of the Condominium was a very important one, justifying at this stage this community being over-represented in relation to its percentage of overall population. It was also arguable that the knowledge and experience that the majority of the European members could be expected to possess would enable them to give direction to the deliberations of the Assembly, and to constitute a stabilising factor. For reasons which will become apparent later, the principal one being that the NP was unjustly deprived of its majority, the first RA was never really given a chance.

Electoral registration and political developments in Santo and Tanna

Registration of electors for the RA election began in late March 1975 and was completed at the beginning of November, in time for the election to be held during the second week of that month.[15] Although the NP had proposed that

---

15   Keith Woodward, 1978. 'Historical Summary of Constitutional Advance in the New Hebrides, 1954–1977,' 77 typescript pages, Pacific Manuscript Bureau 1151, Canberra, The Australian National University, paragraph 11.

the minimum voting age should be eighteen, the majority of AdCo members were more conservatively minded and the Council recommended that twenty-one should be the minimum voting age. Although AdCo had recommended that expatriates should be permitted to vote in the election for the RA after a minimum period of five years' residence in the Group, the residential qualification which was finally provided for in the Exchange of Notes of 29 August 1975 was three years. Candidates for election were required to be at least twenty-five years of age.

The brevity of the preceding paragraph of my Historical Summary prevents it from conveying an adequate idea of the size of the task of the registration of electors, and its inherent difficulties.[16] The Residencies agreed on two basic principles, namely that as far as humanly possible every political voter should be registered, and that precautions should be taken against electoral fraud. The District Agents in each of the four districts had to organise electoral registration teams, each composed of at least two persons, whose task it was to visit every village and settlement in each of the rural constituencies. They issued electoral cards to every man and woman aged at least twenty-one, and established lists of electors, which were separate for each polling station. When planning this electoral registration programme, in consultation with the District Agents, we realised that a major difficulty for the registration teams would be determining whether young adults had attained the requisite voting age of twenty-one, since the registration of births, deaths and marriages had not been in existence long enough for more than a small number of young children to have had their births officially registered. Though a Joint Regulation providing for the registration of the births, deaths and marriages of New Hebrideans had been issued in 1972 or 1973, the registration teams usually had to accept statements as to age by the person concerned, or from people who knew him or her well. However, if the oral evidence seemed inadequate they could form a rough and ready judgement of age from the appearance of the applicant. Recourse was also had to church baptismal registers or certificates, when these were available. I never enquired to what extent such documentary proof of age was found by the registration teams, but I doubt that it was significant.

The registration teams were mainly formed from District Agency staffs, but teachers were also roped in for the work, where this could be done without detriment to school work. Most of the registration personnel were Melanesian. To minimise the risk of partisan considerations influencing their work, especially where the determination of age was concerned, teams were normally composed of one British and one French Administration employee. As will be seen, allegations were made, especially from the French side, after the elections to the effect that

---

16   Woodward, 'Historical Summary.'

there had been widespread under-age registration for political purposes, but very little evidence of this was adduced, and I was satisfied that the registration teams had done a remarkably good job, often in difficult conditions.

It was fortuitous that by 1975 many villagers throughout the New Hebrides had acquired transistor radios, and thus through this medium, could be informed about the forthcoming elections and the impending arrival in their localities of electoral registration teams. The overwhelming majority of the rural people was very happy to be registered, but I recall there were some Santo bush people who initially declined to accept electoral cards. This was a cause of some concern to the French District Agency at Luganville, as these people, to the extent that they were followers of Jimmy Stevens and Nagriamel, were potential anti-NP voters.

Mention of Nagriamel reminds me that my close involvement in electoral preparations brought about, at some point fairly early in 1975, my one and only visit to Vanafo, jointly with M. Jacques Bonhote, a middle-aged FR officer, to whom Fabre had delegated some of the detailed electoral work. The purpose of the visit was to talk to Jimmy Stevens about the impending constitutional changes, and the importance of Nagriamel participation in the elections. This was not something that could be taken for granted, despite this movement's links with MANH. Although by this time Stevens was already displaying a rather suspicious, not to say hostile, attitude towards the British Administration, and was being assiduously courted by the FR, he received my visit cordially enough. He doubtless remembered my conversations with him at the BR in 1967. As Bonhote had little English and no Bislama, being a recent addition to the FR staff, I did most of the talking. We left Vanafo feeling reasonably satisfied that Stevens would co-operate with the electoral process. I was not to have any conversation with Jimmy again until April 1988, when he warmly welcomed me to his room at the Base Hospital in Port Vila. He was then serving a long term of imprisonment for his role in the failed Vemerama secession attempt in May to September 1980, but was in poor health and died three years later.

I shall venture at this point, since he has come into my narrative, to express a personal opinion about Jimmy Stevens. I think he was genuinely motivated by a wish to prevent further European encroachment on hitherto undeveloped ('dark bush') land when, circa 1964, he and the bush chief Buluk, formed the Nagriamel movement. Although I accept that I could have been misled, because of his plausible charm, I was impressed by his apparent sincerity when he explained the aims of Nagriamel during talks in my office in 1968. Money was his Achilles heel, however, and his desire to acquire it, having been poor all his life, made him vulnerable to exploitation by people wanting to use him for their own ends—financial and political. Thus, for two or three years, beginning in 1968 or 1969, he came under the influence of the shrewd New Caledonian businessman, André Leconte. The latter, desirous of obtaining a large tract of land in south-east Santo for cattle-ranching, persuaded Stevens to accept a deal, which was ostensibly to the mutual benefit of Stevens, his Melanesian followers, and Leconte himself. As I remember it, from the contract that Stevens showed me, Leconte would make his mechanical equipment, bulldozers and trucks, available to the Vanafo people for the clearing of their land, in return for their leasing some 700 hectares to him. I think the ratio was two hectares for one hour of bulldozer, and one hectare for an hour of truck use. *En passant*, it should be noted that most or all of the land to be acquired by Leconte had been adjudicated in 1951 by the Joint Court in favour of SFNH, although the Company's ownership was not, of course, recognised by Stevens and Buluk. I advised Stevens against proceeding with this deal, pointing out that the number of hours for which they would have the use of Leconte's machinery might not be sufficient to clear very much of their land. I asked the Australian lawyer, Harry Wilshire-Webb, to speak to Stevens, and he also advised against implementing the contract. As far as I know, nothing came of it, but Leconte continued to court Stevens for some time, paying for him to visit Noumea, where he was lavishly wined and dined.

By the early 1970s Jimmy Stevens (now often known as Moli, the Santo title of a chief) seemed to have lost sight of the original aims of Nagriamel as a movement of protest against the alienation of land by Europeans. After Leconte, Stevens came under the influence of the American land speculator, Harold Peacock, who presumably saw personal advantage, where his business affairs were concerned, in having Nagriamel on his side. Disastrously, as it proved in the long run for him, the Nagriamel leader also became deeply involved with Michael Oliver and the libertarian members of the Phoenix Foundation.[17]

By the middle of the 1970s, moreover, the FR, which in the 1960s had seen Stevens as something of a bogeyman threatening French economic interests on Santo, had come to regard Nagriamel as an essential element of the anti-NP line-up in the North. I recall being with du Boulay at a meeting with our French colleagues in 1975, when Fabre, rather sheepishly, I thought, revealed the extent of FR material assistance to the Nagriamel settlement at Vanafo.

Stevens, embittered and disappointed by Nagriamel's poor result in the Santo rural constituency election in 1975, proclaimed that Santo would become independent from 1 April 1976 and that the French Administration would be permitted to stay on the island, whilst the British would have to quit. It was to become increasingly obvious, however, as Stevens took Nagriamel out of the mainstream political process into ever closer involvement with the Phoenix Foundation in the late 1970s, that the FR had no control over him. He

---

17   See M. Parsons, 1981, 'Phoenix: ashes to ashes,' *New Internationalist Magazine* 101 (July), online: http://newint.org/features/1981/07/01/phoenix/, accessed 20 July 2014.

had lost touch with reality, which was not, perhaps very surprising, as he was manipulated by the Phoenix Foundation and the leaders of MANH who had themselves little or no understanding of the basic realities of the Condominium. How could, one wonders, either the Phoenix Foundation or MANH have seriously believed that Britain and France would allow them to take Santo out of the New Hebrides/Vanuatu, against the wishes of at least half, probably the majority, of its indigenous population, and turn it into some kind of libertarian paradise?

This may also be the appropriate place to elaborate briefly on the impact of constitutional advance on Tanna. After the adoption of a non-repression approach towards John Frum in the wake of the 1957 marching and drilling episode, the movement was routinely monitored by the District Agents, but left to its own devices. For many years, through the 1960s and into the early 1970s, John Frum posed no threat to public order on Tanna. It could be said, I suppose, that the movement withdrew into itself, displaying a negative attitude towards education, the 1967 census and local councils. In the mid-1970s, however, after the radical activities of the NP had led to the creation of a conservative opposition—UCNH and MANH—encouraged and supported by the FR, a change came about on Tanna. It became the policy of the FR, working through the French District Agent, to foster a group-wide and anti-NP alliance, composed not only of UCNH and MANH, but also of movements rooted in the Melanesian population—Nagriamel and Tabwemasama on Santo and John Frum and Kapiel on Tanna.

The establishment of municipal and community councils

As has been mentioned above, one of the decisions taken at the London Conference of November 1974 was that Municipal Councils should be established for the two towns, together with Community Councils in the rural areas.[18] The establishment of both Municipal and Community Councils was legally provided for in Joint Regulation No.1 of 1975, which prescribed a minimum residential qualification of one year for participation in elections for those bodies. The RCs decided that the Port Vila Municipal Council would be composed of twenty four members (twelve New Hebrideans, six British and six French), to be elected in five wards returning varying numbers of councillors in proportion to their population. Voting would be similar to that prescribed for the RA elections in the two towns, that is, cross-voting with electors being required to vote for at least one British, one French and one New Hebridean candidate in their ward. The Santo (Luganville) Municipal Council was to be composed of sixteen

---

18 Woodward, 'Historical Summary,' para 12.

members (nine New Hebrideans, four French and three British), to be elected by the town as one electoral unit, there being no wards. It should be noted, in view of the subsequent one-sided electoral results—see below—that the BR had pressed for a division of the Municipality into two or three wards, but the FR had adamantly refused on the grounds that the creation of wards would have the effect of further dividing an already divided community. The FR view was reluctantly accepted by the BR, on condition that there should be a New Hebridean majority on the Council, to take account of the fact that the New Hebridean population of Luganville greatly out-numbered the non-native one.

As I have indicated earlier, the purpose of the cross-voting system adopted both for the two urban RA constituencies, and for the Port Vila and Luganville municipal elections, was to ensure a minimum level of non-native, in practice, European, representation on the bodies concerned. I cannot now recall whether cross-voting was an original idea of either Fabre or myself, or was—perhaps more likely—a system that I had heard about from somewhere or other. Another objective, and, I think, of equal importance, was to involve each of the three communities—British, French and New Hebridean—in the election of the representatives of the other two. To some extent, I suppose, it was our conscience salve for requiring a fixed number of European representatives for the two towns, because we could say that the British and French candidates most liked by the New Hebrideans had the best chance of being elected.

The disgracefully one-sided outcome of the Luganville municipal election, which was so unfair to the NP, was so predictable that one must wonder whether FR insistence (for a very feeble reason) on having no wards resulted from mere ineptitude, or their wish to prevent the NP from being properly represented on this council.[19] The quality of those elected to the Luganville Council was poor, and it would have been less dysfunctional had there been a fair level of NP membership.

The elections for both the Port Vila and Luganville Councils were held on 16 August 1975. In Port Vila, eighteen UCNH and six NP Councillors were elected. In Luganville, where there were no wards, fifteen of the Councillors belonged to the MANH/Tabwemasana/Nagriamel (MTN) alliance,[20] hurriedly created for the occasion, and only one to the NP, although the MTN majority was only about 50 per cent of votes cast. This patently unfair result clearly demonstrated the error that had been committed in not dividing the town into wards. As was to be shown again in the urban elections for the RA, the cross-voting system tends

---

19 Woodward, 'Historical Summary,' para 13.
20 These were three very disparate groups with little in common other than their aversion to the NP.

to give the larger party a much greater number of seats than its actual majority in the electorate justifies, unless the town concerned is split into a reasonable number of constituencies or wards.

Brief mention must be made here of the creation in mid-1975 of the Tabwemasana Party, which was to play a part in the confused events of 1976 out of proportion to its numerical importance.[21] This small group was essentially composed of people living in, or originating from, the large Catholic village of Port Olry on the east coast of Santo. Lacking any clearly defined policies, Tabwemasana was even more particularist in outlook than Nagriamel and MANH, its approach being frankly, 'Santo for Santo people'. It is convenient to rectify here the omission to mention earlier the establishment in 1974 of the Natuitano Party, which—like Nagriamel and Tabwemasana—placed much emphasis on the importance of custom and land but which drew its support from the Presbyterian villages scattered around the coast of the island. The Natuitano—which means children of the land—Party was closely associated with the NP from the outset and its candidates for the Assembly stood under NP colours.

Elections

That it proved possible to hold the first-ever universal suffrage elections in the New Hebrides so successfully was due to the hard work and enthusiasm of the very many people concerned in various ways. As I have already indicated, great credit was due to the teams who covered the New Hebrides, often on foot over difficult terrain, registering would-be voters in every village and settlement, no matter how remote and difficult of access. Equal credit was due to the people who also went to every part of the archipelago to set up the polling stations.

It was not, of course, possible in a country like the New Hebrides, to hold the election for the RA everywhere on the same day. There were simply not enough suitable people available to man polling stations simultaneously in every scattered locality, so voting had to be staggered over several days. To avoid the risk (probably only a small one in our political situation) of voters being influenced in their choice by knowledge of voting that had already occurred, the counting of votes did not take place until the sealed ballot-boxes from all the polling stations had been assembled at constituency headquarters, and all voting had ended.

The political parties were entitled to have observers at the polling stations to ensure that no irregularities occurred. In fact, I only heard of one report by a party election observer of attempted electoral fraud. A NP observer at a polling

---

21 Woodward, 'Historical Summary,' para 14.

station in the Santo rural constituency detected an attempt at impersonation, when some Nagriamel supporters, whom the vigilant observer had noticed voting once already, returned to the polling station, and tried to vote with another person's electoral card. I am sure this was an isolated incident, and that the people of the New Hebrides could feel justly proud of the way in which they had exercised their newly-acquired democratic rights, especially as there was such a high turn-out—at least 83 per cent.

Quite a lot of special joint legislation governing the conduct of the elections had to be brought into force in 1975, and usually as quickly as possible. I was fortunate in that once it had been agreed with our French colleagues what should be put in the various pieces of legislation, which was generally not difficult, I could turn to Paul Threadwell Q.C., the BR's Attorney-General, and ask him to do the necessary legal drafting. He was always very helpful and willing to give my work priority. It was a considerable advantage to have this electoral legislation initiated by a good legal draftsman on the British side. The FR did not have an equivalent to Threadwell, and since Jacques Fabre was always over-worked, there would have been more delay in bringing out legislation if we had had to wait for it to be originated by the FR. Then I would have had to translate it, and hope that it would not be too difficult for Paul Threadwell to produce a satisfactory English text, once we were happy about the substance. It so happened that Mr. Gordon Norris, an Administrative Officer who had joined the BR from Malaysia in 1970, carried out periods of duty as British District Agent in a relieving capacity in three of the four districts during 1975, beginning with CD1 and going on to Central District No. 2 (Malekula, Ambrym, Pentecost and Paama) (CD2), and ending the last few months of the year in Northern District (Santo, Ambae, Maevo, Banks and Torres) (ND).

I have always said, and this with all due respect to the abilities of the substantive occupants of the districts concerned, that it was fortunate, where the organisation of the registration of electors was concerned that Norris spent some time in CD2 and ND during the middle and latter part of 1975. He had a considerable talent for detailed organisational work and he judged, rightly, that preparation of the elections should be his first priority, while he was in those districts, rather than normal administrative work. Another valuable contribution made by Norris to the efficient conduct of the elections was the drawing up of detailed instructions for Polling Officers. His grasp of detail enabled him to make these instructions a model of comprehensiveness and clarity.

Elections for the first RA were held during the first half of November 1975.[22] These included not only the polling—spaced over a week or more in some parts of the Group—for the twenty-nine universal suffrage seats, but also those for

---

22   Woodward, 'Historical Summary,' para 15.

the six members representing the Chamber of Commerce section of Economic Interests and the three New Hebrideans representing the Co-operative Societies. However, of the four Chiefs provided for in the Exchange of Notes of 29 August 1975, only two were elected during this period, for CD1 and CD2. In the case of the latter district, the election of Chief Willie Bongmatur of North Ambrym was disputed. The District Agents for the Northern and Southern Districts had not been able to constitute the Electoral Colleges for their districts. In the ND this failure was due in part to the burden of having to arrange the elections for the Luganville Municipal area and then the RA in quick succession, but partly also to the differences of view between the District Agents as to the manner in which the Electoral College should be constituted. In the Southern District (SD) the lack of any clearly defined system of chieftainship on the principal island of Tanna was the major obstacle to the rapid establishment of the chiefly Electoral College, but here also political factors were present. Whilst it had originally been hoped, probably by both the New Hebrideans and by the Government, that the election of chiefs would not be a political matter, the general political situation had evolved so rapidly between January and November 1975, that politicisation of the chiefly elections had become more or less inevitable by the latter date. It must regretfully be acknowledged that realisation of the effects that the results of the chiefly elections might have had on the general political balance in the RA influenced the attitudes and actions of some district agents during this period.

The realisation of the possible political importance of the two chiefly elections remaining to be held was greatly heightened when the results of the universal suffrage and other elections for the RA were assessed by the politicians.[23] Of the twenty-nine universal suffrage seats, seventeen were won by the NP—a success which even its most optimistic supporters had hardly considered possible— ten were captured by UCNH and the remaining two by Nagriamel/MANH. Since the two Chiefs already elected to represent CD1 and CD2 were known NP supporters, and two of the three Co-operatives' representatives belonged to that party, it became obvious that the question as to whether or not the NP would have a majority of one or even two seats in the Assembly depended on the results of the chiefly elections to be held in the SD and ND.

The results of the elections for the RA came as a shock to the FR, as they did of course, to the opponents of the NP. They had expected the NP to be in a minority of one seat only in both the Santo rural and the Luganville constituencies. Instead, Walter Lini's party had won four of the six Santo seats. The alarm that the results created in the FR was so great that the FRC (M. Robert Gauger, who had succeeded Langlois earlier in the year) hurried down to discuss the situation with his British colleague. The latter, Mr. John Champion, had succeeded du Boulay just a few weeks earlier, and thus had very little time to become properly

---

23   Woodward, 'Historical Summary,' para 16.

acquainted with the politics of the Condominium. Like du Boulay, Champion had begun his career in the Colonial Service, but had transferred to the Foreign Service in the 1960s. He was a man of considerable ability and charm, but lacked the toughness that had stood his predecessor in good stead in dealing with French colleagues intent on pursuing their own political agenda.

The purpose of Gauger's urgent meeting with his new British counterpart was to discuss the situation created by the NP's unexpected measure of success, and what could be done to minimise its political consequences, if possible. Champion told me afterwards that Gauger was looking for some way of preventing the NP from obtaining an overall majority in the Assembly. It was my impression that the FRC's approach had brought Champion up against the sordid realities of the Condominium with something of a shock. He had, of course, no solution to offer to his worried colleague. I regret to have to record that from this point onwards, the FR devoted much energy to finding a way, or ways, of preventing the NP from obtaining even the most slender majority in the Assembly. This would be done on two levels. The best efforts of the French District Agents in the SD and ND would be directed to ensuring that the chiefly electoral colleges of these districts had anti-NP majorities. As will be evident in the following pages, the inability of the British and French District Agents in the ND to submit to the RCs agreed recommendations for the composition of the chiefly electoral colleges for their district was to delay the first meeting of the fully-constituted RA until almost the end of 1976. There was much less delay in the submission of jointly agreed recommendations for the SD electoral college, which occurred in February 1976, probably because the French District Agent, M. André Pouillet, with his eight years of experience on Tanna, was able to exert greater influence on the composition of the college than his British colleague. The latter was on a brief posting to the district, and had no previous direct knowledge of it, having been taken out of the Secretariat to spend the first few months of 1976 on Tanna because no one with experience in SD was available. This is not to say, however, that the composition of the electoral college would have been much different had, say, Gordon Norris, been British District Agent of the SD at the time, given that NP supporters were in the minority among traditional leaders on Tanna. I certainly was not sorry that the chief elected to represent the Southern District was not a NP man, given that the party won the other three Districts.

The success of the Natuitano Party in winning all three seats in the Santo urban, or Luganville constituency, and two of the three in Santo rural, came as a very disagreeable surprise to both the French opposing the MTN alliance and to the FR. The latter was convinced that Natuitano/NP had achieved this success through electoral fraud, especially by the registration of under-age voters and by moving NP supporters into Luganville shortly before the elections, so as to boost their voting strength in the urban constituency

The electoral legislation brought into force in 1975 provided for the establishment of an electoral commission, and for the submission to it of petitions if disputes arose over the results of elections. The FR, however, could have had little confidence in the ability of the MTN alliance in Santo to prepare the evidence required to support electoral petitions challenging the election of five Natuitano/NP Assembly Members for the two Santo constituencies. The French District Agency at Luganville had its work cut out to keep the fragile electoral alliance together, and there were few, if any, well-educated people in MANH, the only component with a European membership. There is strong circumstantial evidence that the French Administration at the very least helped in the preparation of the MTN's electoral petitions, because a FR official removed various electoral registration lists from the Condominium Electoral Offices in Port Vila. Detailed study of the relevant lists of electors would have been essential to the preparation of electoral petitions challenging the Natuitano/NP wins in the two Santo constituencies.

I departed from Port Vila in December 1975 for three months leave in England. I was allowed to take this leave before reaching the end of a normal two-year tour of duty, in view of the intensity of the work I had been engaged in during the preceding year.

Bringing the Representative Assembly into existence

At this point in the account of constitutional and political events in the New Hebrides, I am obliged to rely, in describing what happened in 1976, on the relevant paragraphs of my Historical Summary.[24] This is because I have no detailed memory of my personal involvement in the protracted negotiations, both inter-Residency, and with the political parties, which are summarised in the following paragraphs. This was probably due to my inability to exercise any significant personal influence on the course of events, although it was not for the want of trying. The year 1976 was frustrating for me, and no doubt for everybody else who had worked hard in 1975 to bring the RA into existence, only to see its first meeting endlessly delayed by political manoeuvring. This unhappy situation came about, essentially, because the NP had done so unexpectedly well in the elections, and for its opponents some way had to be found to prevent it having an overall majority in the RA. Henceforth, the political scene was to be dominated by the conflict between the NP and its various opponents, not the

---

24 Woodward, 'Historical Summary.'

least of which was the French Administration. The BR, having no political axe to grind, but anxious to see the Assembly functioning as soon as possible, did its best to play the part of an honest broker.

The Nagriamel/MANH group was deeply disappointed by the results of the RA elections, particularly in the island of Santo, where they obtained only one seat instead of the majority, which they expected.[25] The leaders of this group filed petitions against the elections of the NP members for both the Santo rural and Luganville constituencies. In the first half of December, Nagriamel staged two large demonstrations in Luganville in support of these electoral petitions. The American land speculator, Eugene Peacock gave Jimmy Stevens considerable help in transporting Nagriamel members, both from other islands to Luganville and from points inland on Santo to that town, for the second and larger of these demonstrations.

On 27 December 1975, a third and even larger Nagriamel/MANH demonstration was held in Luganville. On this occasion, Stevens presented to the public two documents formally proclaiming the immediate independence of the newly-named Nagriamel Federation (NGF), the territorial area of which would comprise the island of Santo (excluding the town of Luganville) together with nearby islands, including Ambae and Maevo and the Banks and Torres Group. These proclamations were signed by Jimmy Moli Stevens in his capacity as President of the NGF on behalf of the Federation's 'Upper Council'. A third document, also signed by Aimé Maleré, the President of MANH, summoned the British Administration to leave Santo by 1 April 1976, since it had contributed nothing to the development of the island and was considered to be hostile to its further progress, whilst the French would be permitted to remain subject to conditions to be defined later. The British Administration was requested, moreover, to arrange for Condominium Services to be transferred to the French. On 29 December, however, Stevens requested the RCs to consider the documents proclaiming the immediate independence of the NGF to be replaced by a new declaration. This document, which was signed only by Stevens, although it purported to have been drawn up in agreement with MANH, stated that the island of Santo, including Luganville, together with any other islands wishing to join it, would become independent from 1 April 1976, on which date the NGF would regard the Anglo-French Protocol of 1914 as having ceased to be operative. As in the earlier document signed by both Stevens and Maleré, this new declaration required the British Administration to quit Santo on 1 April, the French being permitted to remain, as envisaged before. Apart from the three months postponement of the coming into force of the Nagriamel declaration of

---

25 Woodward, 'Historical Summary,' para 17, followed by paras 18 and 20–28. These paragraphs are presented in this section of the book.

independence and the fact that Luganville would also be covered by it, the main other difference was that the islands of Ambae, Maevo and the Banks and Torres Group were not specifically included in the area to become independent.

Whilst the two documents of 27 December proclaiming the immediate independence of the NGF were recognisably inspired by either Peacock or Oliver, the two documents issued on behalf of both MANH and Nagriamel, in which the British Administration was required to leave Santo by 1 April, may have owed more to the influence of anti-British elements amongst the French population of Santo than to the two Americans, although neither Peacock nor Oliver had any reason to like the British Administration. Bearing in mind that Peacock had already left the New Hebrides on 19 December and Oliver on 25 December, it is possible that by 29 December MANH's influence over Stevens had to some extent replaced that of the absent Americans and that the significant changes in the Nagriamel independence programme were due to this factor. Be this as it may, American influence on Nagriamel subsequently declined (neither Peacock nor Oliver being permitted to return to the New Hebrides) and was gradually replaced by the influence of the FR, although this did not again become effective (and possibly to a lesser extent than in 1974–75) until several months had elapsed.

On 31 December 1975, the RCs reacted to the Nagriamel bombshell by issuing a communiqué which rejected the right of any one political party to speak for all or any part of the New Hebrides, and pointed out that for either of the two powers to relinquish its responsibilities for the whole or any part of the Group would be in conflict with the Protocol. They also affirmed that the question of independence was one for decision by the Metropolitan Governments in consultation with local political leaders, especially the members of the RA. For the RCs, the next few months were to be dominated by two main preoccupations: one was the need to prevent Nagriamel secession and to bring Stevens and his followers back into the normal political arena (and, if possible, Stevens himself into the Assembly); the other was to find a way of completing the election of chiefs to the RA on a basis which would be satisfactory to the political parties.

It will be recalled that only two of the four chiefs had been elected in November 1975 and that a bitter political dispute had arisen over the election of one of these, Chief Willie Bongmatur of North Ambrym. The RCs had originally hoped that the new Assembly would be able to hold its first meeting not later than early December 1975 and that, after having got through such preliminaries as the adoption of Standing Orders and the election of committees, it would shortly afterwards be in a position to undertake consideration of the 1976 Condominium Budget. These hopes were dashed by the non-election of the chiefs for ND and SD and, leaving aside the possibility that until these chiefs had been elected the

Assembly might not be legally properly constituted, the fact that neither the NP nor UCNH were willing to sit down in the Assembly until all its members had been chosen.

It has been mentioned earlier that disagreement between the District Agents concerned as to the manner in which the ND and SD Chiefly Electoral Colleges were to be constituted had been one of the causes of the delay in the election of chiefs to represent the Districts in the Assembly. The Exchange of Notes of 29 August 1975 had not attempted to lay down precise rules for the composition of the Electoral Colleges; it simply required the District Agents in each District to make recommendations to the RCs who would then appoint the members of each College by Joint Decision. This lack of detailed provisions was not due to an oversight, but rather to the fact that the structure of Melanesian society differed from District to District and from island to island, with the result that there was no uniform system of chiefly authority and that no precise rules as to the manner of setting up the Electoral Colleges would be valid for each District. Nevertheless, the proposition can be fairly advanced that, if the representation of the chiefs in the Assembly had not become such a politicised matter, the setting up of adequately representative Electoral Colleges for each District would not have presented a major problem. This view is supported by the fact that the District Agents for CD1 and CD2, acting in concert with leading New Hebridean personalities (especially men who were recognised to be chiefs or to possess equivalent authority), had been able to submit to the RCs agreed proposals for the composition of their respective Electoral Colleges which were generally acceptable in mid-1975, before it was realised that the political composition of the Chiefly Section of the Assembly would be such a crucial matter.

In the first half of December 1975, the RCs held consultations with members of UCNH and other local politicians (but the NP refused to take part) in an attempt to obtain political agreement as to the manner in which the two remaining chiefly Electoral Colleges should be chosen. Following these consultations, fairly detailed instructions were sent to the District Agents in the districts concerned requesting them to undertake an elaborate process of consulting people, especially those with knowledge of custom, in the various parts of their districts with a view to the submission of generally accepted names for the appointment of the outstanding Electoral Colleges. The District Agents had not been able to embark on the consultations, however, when the crisis precipitated by the Nagriamel declaration of independence broke at the end of the year. The task of completing the Chiefly Section of the Assembly soon became complicated by considerations arising from the threat of Nagriamel secession. Preoccupied with the need to find a way of bringing Stevens into the Assembly and realising that the chances of his being elected as the chief to represent ND were virtually non-existent, the RCs proposed that the number of chiefs should be increased from four to eight, a measure which could be expected to enable the political minorities in each district to be represented in the Assembly by chiefs of their own persuasion. This proposal was submitted to the political parties, including the NP, by the French High Commissioner in February 1976 and first reactions to it appeared to be not unfavourable. However, despite efforts made by the Foreign and Commonwealth Office and the French DOM/TOM (the Ministry dealing with New Hebrides affairs) during visits made by Father Walter Lini and Pastor Fred Timakata—respectively the President and Vice-President of the NP—to London and Paris in March 1976, the NP decisively rejected the proposal to increase the number of chiefs and on 27 March 1976, staged demonstrations in each of the main centres in the New Hebrides demanding the early constitution of the Assembly on the basis of the 1975 Exchange of Notes. Of these demonstrations, the one held in Luganville was marred by an unprovoked attack on the peacefully marching demonstrators by members of the Tabwemasana Party—an incident which considerably increased the bitterness of New Hebridean politics.

Although the approach of 1 April, the date fixed three months earlier by Nagriamel and MANH for the independence of Santo caused considerable apprehension among non-Nagriamel inhabitants of Luganville and the rural areas of Santo, the day itself passed off without incident. In the event, Stevens contented himself with sending a deputation of Nagriamel chiefs to deliver a document to the District Agents at Luganville in which it was stated that the date of independence for Santo had been postponed until 10 August, the day of the traditional annual Nagriamel celebrations at Vanafo. This change of plan can probably be ascribed to the precautions taken by the Joint Administration, including the sending of British and French police reinforcements to Santo in order to prevent any move by Nagriamel against Luganville for the purpose of marking the independence of the island. The step backwards may have been due, it must be admitted, as much to the threat of an attack on Vanafo by Tabwemasana (made known a few days earlier) as to prudence resulting from the preparations by the Government. Indeed by 1 April 1976, Stevens and Nagriamel were without allies on Santo since by that time their previously staunch partner, MANH, had formally dissociated itself from the intended secession. During the next few months the line taken by Stevens and Radio Vanafo (the illegal transmitter given to him by the American, Michael Oliver) was isolationist: Nagriamel wanted nothing to do with the Condominium and, in particular, regarded the RA as entirely irrelevant to its needs.

In the meantime, efforts continued in Port Vila to resolve the problem of the representation of chiefs in the RA. Following a meeting between the RCs and

NP leaders on 12 April, it was provisionally agreed—subject to the approval of the Metropolitan Governments—that a meeting of RA members, on an informal basis not constituting an official session of the Assembly, would be held on 29 April in order to find a solution to the problem. In the event, however, the NP boycotted this meeting, on the grounds that the two Governments had not indicated their agreement to it by the 20 April deadline previously set by the party for a decision on the issue of chiefly representation. The meeting of 29 April was attended by the UCNH/MANH members of the Assembly and the representatives of Economic Interests (Chamber of Commerce), together with a number of custom chiefs in the capacity of observers, the latter having been invited by UCNH before obtaining the RCs' consent. This meeting resulted in the adoption of a motion to the effect that ten chiefs should be elected to the RA, one for each of the major islands or groups of islands. The impasse was only broken when, following discussions between the British High Commissioner (Mr. H. Stanley) and NP leaders during the former's visit to Port Vila in early June 1976, the NP agreed to take part in a special meeting of the RA to be convened for the sole purpose of discussing the question of chiefly representation. The first session of the RA, which met with no chiefs present (it having been agreed between the Joint Administration and the political parties that the two chiefs already elected should not take part) began on 29 June 1976.

Of the two MANH/Nagriamel members of the RA, one—the local Frenchman, Michel Thevenin—only put in a brief appearance at the first session, and then only for the purpose of denouncing its proceedings, and the other—Thomas Tungu (from Ambae)—did not arrive until the third and last day of the meeting. Tungu's attendance was at variance with Radio Vanafo's announcement that Nagriamel would boycott the Assembly in accordance with its secessionist policy of the previous few months. It is not clear to what extent Tungu's belated presence represented an initial, but only partial, success for persistent FR efforts to bring MANH/Nagriamel back into the normal political arena.

The principal results of the first session were first, that the adoption by nineteen votes to fourteen, with M. Delacroix. M. Bacon and M. René Ah Pow of the Economic Interests section abstaining, of a NP motion that there should be only four chiefly seats in the Assembly (as already provided for in the Exchange of Notes of 29 August 1975) and, second, a laboriously negotiated NP/UCNH joint motion, supported by thirty-six of the thirty-seven members present, to the effect that a Council of Chiefs should be set up to advise the RA on all matters concerning custom. UCNH announced that it would abide by the Assembly's vote in favour of maintaining the number of chiefly seats in the Assembly at four. In view of this decision, it was virtually a foregone conclusion that both Metropolitan Governments would confirm the Assembly's proposal.

The way was not yet clear, however, for the full RA to begin its work. Apart from the fact that the chiefs to represent ND and SD had still to be elected (and, in the case of ND, the composition of the Electoral College still to be recommended by the District Agents to the RCs), by-elections had to be held for the filling of five seats vacant in the two Santo constituencies. Early in May 1976, the Electoral Disputes Committee (EDC) had declared its decision regarding the petitions and counter-petition presented by Nagriamel and the NP in respect of the election results in Santo and Port Vila. The Committee rejected the NP petition against the election of the six UCNH members for Port Vila and declared invalid the election of all three members representing Santo rural, together with one of the three members representing Luganville, on the grounds of various irregularities, including voting by small numbers of under-age electors. The NP appealed to the Joint Court to reverse the EDC's decision in respect of its unseated Santo members, but the Court in judgements delivered in July 1976 upheld the EDC's decision regarding the three Santo rural seats and, furthermore, annulled the election of the French NP member for Luganville as well as that of British NP member, Mrs. Mary Gilu.

Annulment of Santo elections and by-elections

The decision by the Joint Court[26] to uphold the ruling of the EDC with regard to the Santo rural seats, but also to annul a second Luganville seat (in addition to the one already invalidated by the EDC) was portentous in its political consequences, and merits examination here. Mr. Justice (later Sir) Renn Davis came in person to my office immediately after the Joint Court appeal sitting to inform me of the Court's judgement, for which he apologised. I do not know whether the apology was indicative of misgivings on his part regarding the judgement.

When considering the Joint Court's ruling on the Luganville election, it should be borne in mind that the Joint Court had not, since 1939, been constituted as envisaged by the Protocol of 1914 with a President and the British and French judges. When the second and last Spanish President, Senor Bosch-Barrett, had gone on leave in 1939, the British and French Governments decided that the Condominium should be spared the expense of a President of the Joint Court, and Bosch-Barrett was not allowed to resume his functions, much to his disappointment. He had, like his predecessor, the Conde de Buena Esperanza, been appointed by the King of Spain, but by 1939 General Franco was in power,

---

26 M. Louis Cazendres, the French judge, and Mr. Justice Dermot Renn Davis, the British judge.

and this change of regime may also have been a factor in the decision of the Metropolitan Governments to dispense with a President of the Joint Court. However, this is mere speculation on my part. An Exchange of Diplomatic Notes of 1939 between the two Condominium Powers provided for the Joint Court to be in future constituted by the British and French Judges, who would sit with an Assessor, the latter to have a consultative voice. At some point in the 1960s, the then British and French judges, Mr. Justice James Trainor and M. Le Juge Georges Guesdon, formally pointed out to the RCs the difficulties under which they laboured in the absence of a President. They therefore proposed that they should be appointed Joint Presidents, and should in consequence receive additional remuneration. This proposal was rather reluctantly accepted, despite some scepticism on the parts of the RCs, since the Court had apparently functioned well enough for more than twenty years without a President. Normally, of course, political considerations would not intrude upon the deliberations of the Joint Court, but it had not had to adjudicate on an electoral dispute. Given the politically charged atmosphere of 1976 in the New Hebrides, I cannot exclude the possibility that the two judges disagreed on political lines, and that Judge Davis gave way, against his better judgement, to pressure from the French judge, where the Luganville election was concerned, so that the Court could reach a decision. This, again, is speculation on my part, and—as both men are dead—we shall never know how they deliberated in this difficult case.

The by-elections resulting from the Joint Court's appeal judgements were held at the end of October 1976; the NP retained its two Santo Rural seats, but lost one of the three seats it had previously held in Luganville, its sole French member of the Assembly (Philibert de Montgremier) being ousted by MANH candidate, Georges Cronsteadt. Perhaps the most significant feature of the Santo by-election was the decision by the Nagriamel movement to participate, despite the frequently repeated denunciations of the Assembly by Radio Vanafo during the first half of 1976 and its proclaimed secessionist policy. This reversal of attitude was only brought about after months of unremitting efforts by the French Administration and can probably be regarded as a personal triumph for the then French District Agent, M. Lefilatre. Moli Stevens, replaced M. Michel Thevenin as the movement's member for Santo Rural. The retention of the NP of its two Santo Rural seats, despite the fact that it did not have a majority in the electorate, was mainly due to the splitting of the anti-NP vote by the participation in the contest of Tabwemassana and Fren Melanesian party candidates, in addition to Stevens and Tangis Buluk (see Table 1). Voting figures were:

Table 1. The retention by the NP of its two Santo Rural seats, despite the fact that it did not have a majority in the electorate, was mainly due to the splitting of the anti-NP vote by the participation in the contest of Tabwemassana and Fren Melanesian party candidates.

Candidate	Votes
Thomas Reuben (NP)	1126
Jimmy Stevens (NG)	977
Titus Path (NP)	887
Tangis Buluk (NG)	869
Etienne Poune Narae (Tabwemasana)	462
Albert Ravutia (Fren Melanesian)	275

Source: Author's compilation.

The participation in the Luganville by-election of a Tabwemassana candidate also prevented MANH from gaining the British seat in that constituency, although the NP did not have a majority, its voting strength in the town having declined slightly since the 1975 General Election.

The fact that the NP lost only one seat in the Luganville by-election, and retained the two seats that it had won in the Santo rural constituency indicated that the poor showing of its opponents was due more to the inability of the latter to present a united front in both the 1975 and 1976 elections than to any electoral fraud or sharp practice by the NP. The NP retained its two seats in Santo Rural because, unlike the badly organised MTN alliance, its leaders realised that if the party fielded three candidates, in what would have been a futile attempt to win all three seats, they would risk winning only one, or even none at all. This realisation was presumably based on examination of the voting figures for the constituency in the 1975 general election, from which they would have deduced that Natuitano was not in a majority in the constituency. The MTN had enough electoral support to win three seats and would have done so, if it had not put up three candidates—or four if Fren Melanesian (FM) regarded itself as an ally of MTN—a point that I am not sure about. As it was, the participation of an FM candidate made the Natuitano victory even more certain.[27]

My colleagues in the FR were convinced that the NP/Natuitano deliberately moved supporters from other island constituencies into Luganville in the weeks preceding the 1975 election, in order to take advantage of the provision in the law for late transfer of registration, and by so doing to swell their voting strength in Santo Urban. Whether this was the case I do not know, but I very much doubt

---

27   A small party, drawing its support in South Santo and North Malekula from the French Protestant sect led by Pastor Charlemagne, who lived in New Caledonia. Its candidate in the by-election, Albert Ravutia, was to hold office briefly in the first Council of Ministers under George Kalsakau in 1978.

it. To perform such a piece of electoral engineering, the party would have had to balance the possible, but by no means certain, gain to be had in Luganville against the risks involved in weakening its voting strength elsewhere, despite lacking adequate population data.

Because of his belief that the NP had engineered the Luganville election, my then colleague in political matters at the FR, M. Francis Doyen, who had succeeded Fabre as Chancelier in 1976, insisted on amending the electoral legislation in advance of the Santo by-elections, so as to prevent late transfer of electoral registration. It was agreed that there should be a mandatory period of six months' residence for electoral registration, as was the law in France. It was obvious to me from Doyen's rather aggressive attitude when this matter was discussed, that the FR was prepared to make a major issue of it. I could not advance any strong argument against the six months' residence requirement, and I did not expect the BRC, Mr. John Champion, would wish to quarrel with the FR on the point, especially as our principal concern in 1976 was how to expedite the first meeting of the then still incomplete RA. As has been mentioned earlier, two of the Assembly's four chiefs had still not been elected, and would not be until November of that year.

The loss, in the October 1976 by-elections of one of their three seats in the Santo urban constituency by the NP, whilst resulting in a politically more equitable representation of Luganville, was to bring about the premature and inglorious end of the first RA in February 1977. This was due to the resentment felt by the NP in having been deprived, by losing their seat in Luganville, of the majority of one which it would otherwise have held in the Assembly. The NP leaders could not but unreasonably feel that the structure of the Assembly had been weighed against them from the outset. It was significant that one of the party's demands in February 1977 was to be the removal of the Chamber of Commerce members from the Assembly, the rejection of which resulted in the NP's boycott of the RA and its subsequent collapse. The inclusion in the RA of these six members, officially styled 'representatives of Economic Interests', rendered nugatory the substantial majority of five seats won by the NP in the universal suffrage election.

It was clear to me from Doyen's attitude during our discussions of the amendment to the electoral legislation in preparation for the Santo by-elections, that he thought the NP enjoyed the covert support of the BR. He made plain his dislike and distrust of that party on many occasions. This attitude on Doyen's part, which no doubt reflected the feelings of the FR in general towards their British colleagues, could, I think, in large measure have been due to the curious, and unfortunate situation of the BR vis-à-vis the NP.

A Political Memoir of the Anglo-French Condominium of the New Hebrides

Origins and perceptions of the National Party

This situation derives from the NP's origins, and the composition of its leadership. As late as ten years before independence, and apart from a small number of Anglican priests and Presbyterian pastors, the largest number of fairly well-educated New Hebrideans were to be found in the British National Service (BNS), of which the BRC was the head. It was not surprising therefore, that the founding fathers of the New Hebrides Cultural Association, which began life early in 1971, were senior Melanesian members of the BNS. Within a few months, the Association became the New Hebrides NP, and had held its first public demonstration in support of the Joint Administration's policy of controlling subdivisions, a matter to which I have referred earlier. From the outset, the BR's position was that it should do nothing to inhibit the development of a political party by New Hebrideans. I knew that my good friend and colleague the late Dick Hutchinson had given some guidance to either Peter Taurakoto or Donald Kalpokas,[28] perhaps both, who were BR Assistant Education Officers, regarding the formation of the Cultural Association. I also remember George Kalkoa (later Sokomanu) asking me to look at a draft constitution for the NP. He was then an Assistant Administrative Officer in the British Service.

By the mid-1970s, when the NP was growing increasingly insistent in its demand for early independence—its stated target for that event being 1977—most but not all of the New Hebridean members of the British Service were enthusiastic NP supporters, and some of the senior ones were on its committee. The FR and the public at large were, of course, well aware of this.

Although, as I have indicated above, individual BR officers, including myself, gave a little advice and mild encouragement to various New Hebrideans when the NP was being set up, I am in a position to state categorically that at no time did the BR exercise any control over, or have improper involvement with this party. I often had cause to regret that we had virtually no influence over the leadership of the NP, although there were occasions when I tried to take advantage of my friendly relations with most of them individually to divert them from extreme courses of action. One of these occasions was when I went out to Mele to see Ati George Kalkoa in his house, in a fruitless attempt to avert the NP demonstrations of 27 December 1973 at the FR, already mentioned in these pages. There was another instance in 1977 when I provided cold Fosters (beer) in my house to many of the NP leaders in what proved to be a vain hope of influencing them towards a more flexible attitude on some matter which I have

---

28   R.J.S. Hutchinson served variously as BDA CD1, CD2 and ND between 1956 and 1972. While on Santo, he played a big part in bringing to justice Taptapus, Tapun and the thirty-two other Big Bay bush murderers, for which he received insufficient recognition. See Hutchinson, 2002, 'Dick Hutchinson: Administrative officer 1956–1972,' in *Tufala Gavman: Reminiscences from the Anglo-French Condominium of the New Hebrides*, ed. B.J. Bresnihan and K. Woodward, Suva: Institute of Pacific Studies, University of the South Pacific, pp. 301–26.

now forgotten. The inescapable fact was that in 1976 and 1977, the NP leadership was embittered by the loss of its majority in the first RA, and no longer trusted the Joint Administration. The party knew that the FR was working against it, and had no confidence that the BR could, or would, do anything for it.

That the general public in the New Hebrides, and particularly the French community, saw the relationship between the NP and the BR in quite another light was brought home to me in various ways. Early in 1975, after he had attended some social function, the then BRC, Roger du Boulay, told me that the American manager of a formerly French-owned plantation had remarked that he knew me to be 'the President of the NP'. The formerly very friendly relations that I had enjoyed with French planters on Efate cooled noticeably, and I was never invited by M. Gauger (FRC 1975–77) to any FR social function other than the Quatorze Juillet (July 14th) cocktail party attended by *le tout Port-Vila* (all of Port Vila). In 1980, after I had left the New Hebrides, a French woman (a cousin of the well-known businessman, Pierre Bougeois) said to me in a very friendly way, '*Je sais que vous avez fondé le Vanuaku Party (VP)*' (I know that you founded the Vanuaku Party).[29] These words were spoken to me, in a very friendly manner by Martine Rundle, who had married an old school fellow of mine, at the time Merchandise Manager at Burns Philp & Co, Port Vila. Martine said this to me on an audio-cassette. I did not know her while I was living in Port Vila and she perhaps arrived there after my departure. That she should have thought I had founded the NP/VP revealed the reputation that I had apparently acquired in the French community. The words also showed that many Europeans did not credit New Hebrideans with the ability, unaided by white men, to create and run efficiently, a political party like the NP/VP.

There was, unfortunately, a tendency in the FR to judge their British colleagues, especially where politics were concerned, by their own standard of behaviour. We studiously refrained from any involvement on behalf of the NP during the 1975 electoral campaign. As I have stated earlier, I merely made sure that Kalkot Matas Kele-Kele understood how his party could get maximum advantage from the electoral system that I had originated. He was too intelligent to need telling twice. I would have been very happy to provide UCNH with the same information, but I assumed, quite rightly, that the FR would do that and more. In fact, the FR's support of the so called Moderates (*les modérés*) before the election was quite blatant. I recall there were even allegations that French District Agents were offering some New Hebridean villages material inducement to vote for the Moderates. The French District Agents tried hard, moreover, but without great success to weld the disparate components of the MTN alliance on Santo into an effective opposition to the NP. I suspected that my friend, André Pouillet (French District Agent, SD 1967–77) did much towards getting John Frum to ally itself

---

29 The National Party became the Vanu'aku Pati in 1977.

with UCNH, although the movement had no reason to side with the NP, which it associated with the Presbyterians. In short, the Condominium and with it the *entente cordiale* in the New Hebrides, were not at their best in the mid-1970s.

Distinguishing British and French attitudes and motives

This remaining section of my Condominium memoirs will be different from what has gone before. This is so because, as I have already mentioned, I was able to exercise much less, indeed very little, influence on political and constitutional events during the period 1976–77 than during the years leading up to the Assembly elections of 1975. It is, I think, not too much of an exaggeration to say that the actions of the political parties largely determined the course of events, as described in my Historical Summary,[30] during this period, and beyond. The British and French Governments found themselves reacting to what the parties were doing. Thus, the hopes of the two Governments, that the 1975 elections would be the first stage in a gradual and orderly progress towards self-government, and ultimate independence, were thwarted over the issue of the election of two chiefs to the RA. Moreover, the resentment of the NP over the loss of its majority, following the 1976 Santo by-elections, in the Assembly led to its boycott, and wrecking of it. The party then followed an increasingly hard line, boycotting the second Assembly, setting up its so-called People's Provisional Government, and not coming in from the cold until the second half of 1978, after I had left the New Hebrides. Only then could planned constitutional and political progress be resumed, with the VP and Tan-Union working in collaboration with the British and French Governments. This progress did not remain orderly, however, after the parliamentary elections of 1979, owing to the attempted secession of Vemerana in May–July 1980, but that event lies beyond the scope of this story.

It may help the reader to understand the events of 1976–77 if I try to analyse the attitudes and motives of the various players, the British and French Governments and the political parties, as I saw them at the time, and with the benefit of information that I have acquired since.

British

British Government policy with regard to the Condominium was similar to the one pursued in the other Pacific dependant territories, such as the Solomon

---

30   Woodward, 'Historical Summary.'

Islands and the Gilbert and Ellis Islands, to bring them to self-government and, if they wanted it, independence, by progressive stages. I was asked—in 1962 or 1963—by Sir Michael Gass, then Chief Secretary to the Western Pacific High Commission, to submit my ideas about constitutional advance in the New Hebrides. I clearly recall expressing the view that it was desirable for colonial administrations to institute the process of constitutional advance somewhat ahead of any pressure for it from the people of the territory concerned. I felt, and I do not claim any originality for this idea, that it was preferable to anticipate demand for advance, rather than wait until pressure built up for it, and then, perhaps, be obliged to concede too much too quickly.

In the event, as I have related earlier, the opposition of the French Government, until 1974, to any constitutional change more advanced than the introduction of indirectly elected members to AdCo thwarted the kind of forward-looking policy that I had advocated in the early 1960s. Whether, if we had been able, for example, to set up an elected legislature by 1970, we could have cut the ground from under the feet of Walter Lini, Barak Sope and the other more radical NHNP leaders, one cannot say for sure. However, I feel that the path towards independence could have been smoother, with much less acrimony between New Hebrideans, if a legislative body, based at least in part, on direct elections, had been set up (as was suggested by the British Government, but refused by Paris) by 1970 or 1971.

In venturing this opinion I have a number of factors in mind. One is the fact that, in 1970, the year in which Fiji achieved independence, the Condominium was the only colonial territory in the South Pacific, British or French, not to have some form of elected legislature. New Hebrideans, many of whom by this time had transistor radios, knew what was going on elsewhere in the region, and realised that the Condominium was lagging behind. Another point worth mentioning is that, although anglophone New Hebrideans were the first to set up a political party, the New Hebrides NP, in 1971, there were francophones who also aspired to constitutional advance.

Bearing in mind the points mentioned in the preceding paragraph, I suggest that the history of the last ten years of the Condominium might have been very different if an elected legislature had been set up in 1970 or 1971. Had this been done, that is, had the French Government agreed to do no more in the New Hebrides than it had done already in New Caledonia and French Polynesia, politically-awakening New Hebrideans whether francophone or anglophone, would have had the means of fulfilling their legitimate desire to take a hand in the running of their country. There was, I think, at least a possibility that anglophones and francophones could have worked amicably together towards self-government,[31] and ultimate independence, by progressive stages, on a reasonable time-scale of ten to twelve years. Fifteen would have been preferable, but hardly likely, given that all the former British territories in the South Pacific had attained independence by 1980 or before. There was at least the chance that the NP would not have begun—as it unfortunately did—calling, in 1973/74, for independence by 1977, had its leaders been shown that both Britain and France were willing to give New Hebrideans their say in the process of government.

I do not, however, wish to overstate this line of argument. That Walter Lini was already, by 1974, demanding very early independence was, I am almost certain, due to the young NP (founded only three years earlier, in 1971) having come under external influences. These external influences, such as SPADES would have existed in any case.[32] Leaving speculation aside, it is clear to me that such hope as may have existed in the very early 1970s that anglophones and francophones would not become politically polarised was dashed by the premature radicalisation of the NP, and especially the call for independence in 1977, which alienated the francophones.

SPADES was by no means the only external influence on the NP. The party was in touch with the Black Power movement in the United States, and with the United Nations Committee of Twenty-four, which monitors progress towards decolonisation in the remaining dependent territories, exerting pressure on the colonial nations to speed up the process.[33] The slow rate of constitutional advance in the New Hebrides made the Condominium an obvious target for the Committee. The British Government had traditionally shown itself to be sensitive to its pressure, France much less so.

I have somewhat digressed from the subject of the British Government's policy towards the New Hebrides. A complicating factor in our relations with the FR during most of the 1970s was the fact that many, if not most, of the New Hebridean personnel of the British New Hebrides Service were members of the NP, including some of its leading ones.

---

31 The term francophones should be taken to include various groups or movements of New Hebrideans, such as John Frum and Nagriamel, who were not French-educated, and who were later included with the francophones under the collective term of Modérés or Moderates.

32 South Pacific Action for Development Strategy (SPADES). This organisation, which may have originated in Fiji, although essentially political, operated under a cloak of Christianity, and its promoters certainly included some irresponsible, radical, church leaders, including both Europeans and Pacific islanders. Under the mistaken impression that SPADES was primarily a religious organisation, the BR allowed it to hold a meeting on the British Paddock in 1973, and was subsequently unpleasantly surprised and embarrassed by the highly political nature of the message the speakers had put across. This episode strengthened our French colleagues' suspicion that we in the BR were at best too complacent about the NP's activities, or at worst, supportive of them.

33 In the mid-1970s, the UN Committee of Twenty-four was asking Britain to report progress towards independence for Pitcairn Island! I do not know what response it got from London.

It was the policy of the BR not to prohibit its New Hebridean employees from joining political parties. It seemed preferable to regard membership of the NP, and a reasonable degree of political activity, as normal, rather than to make our staff feel, by dint of prohibition, that we were hostile to party membership and political activity. By 1976–77, however, the BR saw that the time had come to review its policy in this matter. We felt that things were going too far when John Naupa, one of our Executive Officers, took part in an attempt by NP radicals to prevent the deportation of the Black Power activist, Roosevelt Brown, by going to Bauerfield Airport with the intention of physically impeding Brown from being put on an Air Pacific aircraft. We had got wind of this plan, and the NP *coup de main* (helping hand) was foiled by the adoption of my suggestion that the chartered Air Melanesie plane bringing Brown under British Police escort from Ambae should wait at the far end of the runway to allow him to be transferred to the Air Pacific plane when it turned for takeoff. By this means, any serious disorder at the Bauerfield Terminal was averted, although Naupa and others were arrested, and held briefly.

In 1977, the Melanesian personnel of the BR ceased to be permanent and pensionable, and were given contracts. This change was made in the knowledge that, with independence approaching the British Service would only continue for a few more years. At the same time, the opportunity was taken to present those who were the most active NP supporters with the option of resigning from the British Service to become more or less full-time politicians, it being understood that they would have to abandon political activism if they wished to remain in our employment. George Kalkoa was one of those who then left the British Service. Another was our most senior New Hebridean police officer, George Kalsakau. He had been a personal friend since my earliest days in Port Vila, when he had just joined the British Police. So I was rather sad when it fell to me to tell him that he would have to resign if he wished to carry on as one of the principal leaders of the recently formed Natotok Efate Party.[34] I do not recall how many of our New Hebridean staff members left us at this point, but it was only a few, I think.

French

It is now time to look at the FR. When talking about French policy towards the Condominium, it is important to bear in mind that our colleagues looked

---

34 This party, which allied itself with the Modérés, came into being partly in reaction to the NP's apparent attack, later disclaimed, on French education at its mid-1977 congress. Many anglophone New Hebrideans in the Port Vila area sent some of their numerous children to French schools, which were free, as they could not afford to pay the fees to send all of them to English-medium ones. Natotok also resented people from outer islands taking jobs at the expense of Efatese. The party was short-lived, however.

at the New Hebrides from a viewpoint quite different from that of the British Government. This had been the case since the beginning of the Condominium, *mutatis, mutandis...*

There must be a brief sketch of the historical background to the establishment of the Condominium by the Anglo-French Convention of 20 October 1906. It should be noted, and the point is not merely academic, that the word 'Condominium' does not occur in the Convention. Neither does it appear in the amending diplomatic instrument, the Anglo-French Protocol respecting the New Hebrides of 6 August 1914 (brought into force in March 1922). Under the 1906 Convention, the New Hebrides became 'a region of joint influence in which subjects and citizens of the two Signatory Powers shall enjoy equal rights of residence, personal protection, and trade, each of the two Powers retaining jurisdiction over its subjects or citizens, and neither exercising a separate control over the Group' (Article 1 of the 1906 Convention).

By this time, the number of French nationals in the New Hebrides was over twice that of the British population, and the disproportion gradually increased during the early years of the Condominium. There were many more French-owned plantations than British, although the influence over the Melanesian people exercised by the various Protestant Missions (especially the Presbyterians and Anglicans) was much more widespread than that of the Catholic Marist Order, which had begun missionary work much later. Most of the Catholic clergy and nuns were French, and French was taught in Catholic Mission schools.

During the last quarter of the nineteenth century, the Compagnie Calédonienne des Nouvelles Hébrides, founded by the naturalised French citizen, Higginson, and its successor company, SFNH, steadily bought land in the group both directly from Melanesians and from British subjects. By the time the negotiations began between Britain and France which led to the signature of the Convention, at least one-third of the land area of the New Hebrides was under claim of ownership by SFNH. Land was a major issue in the negotiations, with the French Government striving, successfully, to protect the interests of SFNH and the British trying rather ineffectively to ensure that the system of land tenure set up by the Convention did not unduly favour European claimants at the expense of the Melanesians.

It is probable that France regarded the Condominium as an arrangement of a temporary nature, and it may well have hoped, given the increase in French settlement and economic influence, that Britain, which had little direct interest in the New Hebrides, would sooner or later be agreeable to the French acquiring sole control over the group. This was not an unreasonable expectation, since Britain might well have been prepared to agree to French annexation when the question was raised by France in 1885, but for the strong opposition of the

Australian colonies. *Il n'y a que le provisoire qui dure* (Only what is provisional endures). History was to bear out this French maxim. Although various possible alternatives to the continuation of the Condominium were aired during the years immediately following World War I, none was considered feasible. The future status of the New Hebrides was settled when Britain and France at last brought the 1914 Protocol into force in March 1922.[35] The Condominium survived the strains and stresses of World War II, helped by the fact that the French community in the New Hebrides, under the leadership of the FRC, M. Henri Sautot, wisely decided, in July 1940, to rally to General de Gaulle and Free France, before any of the French colonial territories took this step. There was some desultory discussion between the British and Australian Governments beginning in the mid-1950s of the possible take-over by Canberra of Britain's responsibilities in the New Hebrides, but Australia had its hands full in Papua New Guinea, and must have seen little to be gained in acquiring such an unrewarding burden as partnership with France in the Condominium. Anyway, nothing came of it, or was ever likely to. For my part, when I was apprised confidentially of these discussions by the Australian Consul (Dr. Cumpston) when I called on him in Nouméa in 1956, it seemed very unlikely to me that the French would be willing to countenance such a momentous change. Realising that, even if my Resident Commissioner, Mr. (later Sir) John Rennie was privy to the Canberra-London exchanges of views (which I have subsequently learned was the case), he would not want me to be in the know, I subsequently said nothing to anyone upon my return to Port Vila! After all, I was very junior in the BR in those far-off days.

Having written about early French policy towards the New Hebrides, albeit with some degree of digression, I now turn to French policy in the last two decades of the Condominium's existence, the 1960s and 1970s. We are fortunate in having at our disposal a clear exposition of that policy by M. Jacques Mouradian (FRC 1964–69) in his last monthly confidential report to the French Ministry for Overseas Departments and Territories, before leaving Port Vila. Less fortunately, however, I have to rely on fallible memory when referring to it, as I have no recording of this interesting document. As I recall them, the important points in Mouradian's recommendations on French Government policy were as I set them out now.

---

35   Whilst maintaining all the essential features of the 1906 Convention, the Protocol introduced some useful improvements, including provision for setting up the Courts of First Instance and Native Courts, and the appointment of British and French District Agents. Most importantly, from the British viewpoint, was the provision that judgements of the Joint Court, the new Native Courts and the Courts of First Instance would, in future, be executed by joint agreement between the RCs. The Convention had stipulated that each RC should unilaterally carry out Joint Court judgements concerning his own nationals. In practice, as related in Jacomb, 'A Family Portrait,' FRCs failed not infrequently, in the early years of the Condominium, to execute judgements against French citizens convicted of offences against the articles of the Convention regarding the employment of indigenous labourers.

In his report of September or October 1969 Mouradian accepted the inevitability of independence for the New Hebrides, whilst implicitly hoping that it would be sufficiently far in the future for the policy he advocated to have enough time for fulfilment. The cornerstone of this policy was the extension of French influence among the indigenous population, so that, when independence ultimately came, French interests, both economic and cultural, would be preserved subsequently.

As could be expected from the programme of school building in the outer islands that was gathering pace in the 1960s, Mouradian saw education as an essential tool for the extension and deepening of French influence in the New Hebrides. This message was certainly heeded in Paris, judging by the sometimes aggressive way in which French schools were being implanted in the 1970s, with considerable pressure being exerted on villagers to accept them, even where there was an existing English medium school adequate for the number of children. This pressure could lead to friction between villagers opposing the introduction of a new French school, and those in favour of it, as was the case on west Ambrym, at Port Vato, in 1974 or 1975. This dispute reached Resident Commissioner level, and I recall the BRC, Roger du Boulay, taking a firm line with his French colleague, so as to secure the abandonment of the attempt to set up the controversial French school. I also recall the occasion when villagers in west Santo told the Assistant British District Agent that they did not want a consignment of canned food that a French official had left with them as an inducement to accept a French school. Some embarrassment was caused when he tactlessly returned the consignment to the French District Agency![36]

In support of his report Mouradian pointed out that, unlike France, Great Britain had no long-term interests in the New Hebrides, and was anxious, therefore, to divest itself of its responsibilities in the Condominium as soon as possible. It was consistent with this wish that the British were advocating the unification of all public services, including those operated separately by France and Britain, in order to prepare the way for independence. Mouradian urged resistance to this policy, as he saw the continued unilateral operation by France of its health and co-operatives services, which had not inconsiderable impact on the lives of the Melanesians, as another means of maintaining, ever-increasing French influence.

Mouradian's recommendations no doubt found ready acceptance in Paris, where a Gaullist regime, under George Pompidou (who succeeded the General in 1969) was to continue until M. Valéry Giscard d'Estaing was elected President of France in mid-1974. French opposition to constitutional advance was, of course, also maintained during the Pompidou presidency. It was rather ironic that, in

---

36 For further details on this incident see 'Edward Hackford Administrative Officer, 1969-1971 in *Tufala Gavman: Reminiscences from the Anglo-French Condominium of the New Hebrides*, ed. Brian J. Bresnihan and Keith Woodward, Suva: Institute of Pacific Studies, University of the South Pacific, 2002, pp. 276-284.'

1977, Mouradian returned to the New Hebrides to draw up, in conjunction with a British civil servant, proposals for the unification of the national services. By then, of course, the French knew independence was relatively imminent.

A crucial, indeed determining, aspect of the New Hebrides political situation in the mid-1970s was the mistrust, akin to enmity, that existed between the FR, and the French community at large, on the one side, and the NP/VP on the other. I have already mentioned the apprehension felt in the FR and expressed by M. Langlois to Mr. du Boulay and myself in 1974 at the prospect of a NP victory in the forthcoming elections for the RA. There were good reasons for this apprehension. Historically, there was a long tradition of bad feeling between the French in the New Hebrides and the Presbyterian Mission, and the NP, the majority of whose adherents were Presbyterians, saw the French in the same light as the Mission. The land question had a great deal to do with the poor relations between the Presbyterian Mission and the French. The Presbyterian churches in Australia had become alarmed at Higginson's land-buying activities in the last two decades of the nineteenth century, and the Australasian New Hebrides Company had been formed by churchmen in New South Wales to buy land in the New Hebrides to stop it from falling into French hands.[37]

Coming closer to our time, prominent Presbyterian AdCo Members, such as Dr. John Kalsakau and George Kalkoa, were spokesmen in the Council for Melanesian villagers opposing further alienation of land by Europeans, and this opposition gave rise in the 1960s and 1970s to many land disputes, mainly involving French planters or companies seeking to develop land in their registered ownership, or under claim before the Joint Court. Relations between the FR and the NP had been significantly worsened, moreover, by the invasion of the FR grounds on 27 December 1973 by a crowd of NP adherents demanding the release from the French prison in Santo of the Rarua brothers.

As I have mentioned earlier, the success of the NP in the 1975 RA elections was such (and despite the electoral system being designed to ensure it did not win too many seats), that the FR was convinced that the NP must have achieved its results by means of fraud. It seemed to me then that the effect of surprise, which the NP's success had on our French colleagues, was due to failure on their part to appreciate the basic realities of the political situation. The plain fact was that adherents of the various Protestant Missions comprised a substantial majority of the Melanesian population, and that, by 1975, the NP was supported by nearly all of this majority. The only significant exception was the Church of Christ, whose long-time leader on Ambae, Abel Bani, had close links with Jimmy Stevens and the Nagriamel movement, which strongly opposed the NP.

---

37   The assets of the Australasian New Hebrides Company were acquired by Burns Philp & Co in the mid-1890s, and they in turn made over these lands to the Commonwealth Government in 1906, in return for a subsidy to the Burns Philp mail steamers plying between Sydney and the New Hebrides.

I do not know, however, whether all Church of Christ followers on the islands of Ambae, Maevo and Pentecost voted against the NP. In any case, there were enough Anglicans and other NP supporters on these three islands to cancel out Church of Christ votes for the Moderates.

Even if these three islands were taken out of the equation, there were enough adherents of the Presbyterian Church in the rest of the Group, together with the Anglicans in the Banks and Torres Islands, to secure a NP majority in the universal suffrage section of the Assembly, which comprised twenty-nine of the total forty-two seats. It was the apparent failure of the FR to grasp this essential fact, our colleagues' inability to get their electoral sums right, that resulted in their acute disappointment with the result of the 1975 elections. They had obviously expected the loose anti-NP alliance to do very well or even to win. Their failure to do better was due, so the FR assumed, to electoral fraud by the NP. In fact, the Moderates had done about as well, or nearly as well, as I expected them to do, given their electoral potential, in terms of numbers and distribution of their supporters. There was just no possibility of the moderates winning a majority of the universal suffrage seats, unless the NP made a complete mess of organising their voters in the multi-seat constituencies. I admit to having been surprised when this party won all three Luganville, Santo seats. Whether this happened because (as alleged by the French) the NP had deliberately brought supporters into Luganville from other islands so as to increase their voting strength there, I honestly do not know, but they would have only been guilty of electoral gamesmanship because no breach of the electoral legislation would have been involved. Qualified electors were legally entitled, under the 1975 electoral laws, to change their registration from one constituency to another up to quite a short time prior to the date fixed for polling. Fabre and I had provided for this so as to facilitate participation in the elections by as many people as possible.

At some point in 1976, Jacques Fabre, whom I have mentioned fairly often in these memoirs, left the New Hebrides, and was replaced as Chancelier at the FR by Francis Doyen. I had known Doyen since about 1960, and had worked a good deal with him in the early 1960s during the first of his two postings at the FR, and particularly on the preparation of the Joint Labour Regulation. We had a very good relationship during those years, and I assumed that things would be much the same when Doyen became Chancelier. (He had returned to the New Hebrides a year or so earlier, and had held the post of French District Agent CD1 during that time.) Times had changed, however, and things were not the same. The advent of politics, and particularly the success of the NP, with its strident calls for independence, had affected relations between the Residencies. Although, on the surface, my relations with Doyen were cordial, the warmth of the former friendly co-operation in the 1960s had gone. Of necessity, most of our dealings were related to the political situation resulting from the 1975 elections. Doyen's suspicions and dislike of the NP were intense. This had obviously affected his attitude towards me, no doubt because of the belief in French circles that I had close links with the NP, from 1977 the Vanuaku Party (VP).

Relations between the two Administrations reached their lowest ebb at the end of 1977, following a year in which the VP had successively wrecked the first RA, boycotted the Paris Ministerial meeting, refused to take part in the second Assembly and, on 29 November, had declared a 'People's Provisional Government' (PPG). The proclaimed intention of the VP to raise the flag of the PPG in Port Vila, Luganville and other principal centres could have led to violence between that party and the so-called Moderates, had not the VP wisely decided that discretion was the better part of valour, in the face of aggressive mobs of Moderates. Indeed, at about this time, there was an attack on the VP-supporting village of Tautu, north-east Malekula, by people from the Catholic villages of Wala-Rano, who backed the Moderates. There was damage to property, but not to persons.

Opposition to the Vanuaku Party flag-raising ceremony

The date, 29 November 1977, was momentous for me personally and for many other people, including the BRC, John Champion,[38] and two of my BR colleagues. For me, it began before breakfast with a telephone call from Mike Dumper, the British Commandant of Police, who told me he had heard that the Moderates were planning to prevent the VP hoisting its PPG flag at the party's office in the Lo Lam Building on rue Higginson.

I do not remember at what time a crowd of Moderates, mostly francophone New Hebrideans, but also some of the prominent French members of Tan-Union,[39] assembled in the narrow street between the Fung Kwei emporium and the Lo Lam Building. They were certainly there by the time I got to my office, or soon afterwards. I was fortunate in having a reliable source of on-the-spot information, as Tom Bayer, the Manager of PITCO,[40] had his offices in the Lo Lam Building. Through the morning, he kept me in touch by telephone with what was happening below his windows.

---

38   For John Champion's account of the 29th November disturbance see Champion 2002, 'John S. Champion GMG, OBE: British Resident Commissioner, 1975–1978,' in *Tufala Gavman: Reminiscences from the Anglo-French Condominium of the New Hebrides*, ed. B.J. Bresnihan and K. Woodward, Suva: Institute of Pacific Studies, University of the South Pacific, pp. 152–54, pp. 150–51.
39   Formerly called the Union des Communités des Nouvelles-Hebrides or Union of New Hebrides Communities.
40   Pacific Islands Trust Company, one of the numerous financial organisations that had installed themselves in the New Hebrides from 1970 onwards in connection with the euphemistically named Finance Industry or tax haven.

When it was clear that the Moderates were determined to oppose the VP flag-raising, and by force if need be, I telephoned Walter Lini, who at that point (probably between nine and ten o'clock) was still at the Anglican Church in Tagabe, almost two miles from the town centre. I informed him that the Moderates had taken up position in front of the VP office, and urged him to cancel the proposed flag-raising. He was not to be dissuaded, however, and it was not long after our conversation that the VP contingent began its march towards town. I was not particularly surprised by my failure, as Lini no doubt felt the VP would lose face if it was seen to be deterred by the presence of the Moderates at its HQs.

It had been agreed with our French 'partners' that, at either Resident Commissioner or Commandant of Police level, the British and French police forces would co-operate on this day, and that the French would have officers in the British police station in town, so as to facilitate this co-operation. At about mid-morning, however, the French police withdrew, presumably upon instruction from the FR. This was an unfortunate and, indeed, a disastrous let-down on the part of the French. On this, of all occasions, there should have been close co-operation between the two Forces, but there was none, and the British Commandant of Police was left with the option of doing nothing to prevent possibly violent confrontation between the Moderates and the VP, or taking action as he saw fit.

It has to be said that the FR abdicated from its joint responsibility with the BR for maintaining public order in Port Vila on 29 November 1977. I can only ascribe this to its almost pathological dislike of the VP, and apparent willingness to let the Moderates have a free hand against Lini. This view is borne out by their failure to shut down a kind of training camp, which had been set up on French private property near Tebakor, a mile or so north of Port Vila shortly before 29 November. The purpose of this camp was, apparently, to prepare adherents of the Moderates for the use of force against the VP. There can be no doubt that the FR was well aware of its existence. If the VP had been involved in what amounted to para-military training of this kind, which it was not, the BR would have instigated joint action to bring it to an end.

As the morning wore on, and it was reported that the VP contingent from Tagabe was getting steadily closer to the town, the British Commandant of Police became increasingly concerned about the possibility of a violent confrontation between it and the Moderates, who were carrying a variety of weapons. These were mostly clubs and other blunt instruments, but I was informed that the British Police had found a pistol on the ground after the Moderates had initially fled the scene.

As the moment of crisis grew closer, I received two quite agitated telephone calls from Mike Dumper, to the effect that he might have to take action to avert a fracas. I told him I would inform the Resident Commissioner of the situation. When I went into Champion's office, he was on the phone with his French colleague, M. Robert Gauger. It was obvious from the testy way, verging on annoyance, in which he spoke to 'Robby', that there was some disagreement between the two. My surmise was that Champion had complained to Gauger about the withdrawal of the French police, as mentioned above.

When Dumper next phoned me, within minutes of the first call, he made it abundantly clear that he thought the imminent arrival of the VP marchers necessitated urgent action. I cannot recall whether he then mentioned the use of tear gas, but it was possible, or even probable that he did, because I think I was not very surprised, when I heard, a short time later, that it had been fired. I advised Dumper to speak to the Resident Commissioner, as I did not feel able to authorise whatever action he felt was required to defuse the situation. He said that he would speak to Champion.

Dumper must have obtained the Resident Commissioner's covering authorisation to take the action he thought to be appropriate, but neither of them told me what was said when this call took place. Anyway, within a very short time, Tom Bayer phoned me to say the British Police had dispersed the crowd of Moderates with tear gas.

The physical, although not the political, effects of the tear gas were short-lived. After their initial precipitate flight, at least some of the Moderates went the short distance to the British Police Headquarters building and stoned it, with what damage being caused, I did not learn. As tear gas had not, as far as I know, been used in the New Hebrides previously, the element of surprise may have been as significant as any physical discomfort in causing the dispersal of the crowd. Anyway, it was not long, perhaps only ten or fifteen minutes, before Tom Bayer rang me to say the Moderates had re-assembled in front of the Lo Lam building, still determined to deny the VP access to their offices for the flag-raising.

The VP contingent had apparently not been close enough to their goal when the tear gas was fired to take advantage of the temporary absence from the scene of the Moderates to get into the Lo Lam building. When they did finally arrive, a stand-off ensued. No physical confrontation occurred, as the VP, who were unarmed, must have realised that the Moderates were well-placed to prevent the projected flag-raising. Dick Baker, one of my BR colleagues, was asked to go down to rue Higginson, so that he could at least assess the situation and, if need arose, try by his presence to avert disorder breaking out. By this time, late morning, I was too unwell to accompany him, as I had pneumonia, although I did not know it. In any case, my presence would probably not have been appreciated by the Moderate leaders, given my supposed close links with the VP.

In keeping with the apparent decision of the FR to hold themselves aloof from the events of this day, Baker has informed me that no FR officer, or French police were present at the stand-off between the rival groups. After some time had elapsed, Walter Lini decided not to press matters and retired from the scene.

At some point during the lunch-time break, I telephoned the British Base Hospital and arranged to see a doctor. When Dr. Makau Kalsakau examined me, he said that my temperature was 40° centigrade, that I had pneumonia and would have to be hospitalised. So I was absent from my office on that fateful afternoon, and for about a week afterwards.

There are two matters that I should have mentioned earlier in connection with the tear gas episode. The first is that the British District Agent for CD1, Tim Osborne, was with Mike Dumper when the tear gas was fired. To what extent he was involved in the decision to use it, I do not know, as I did not have an opportunity of talking to him after the event, but it is probable that he was consulted. The second is that a man from Tanna, who was in the Moderate crowd, was struck in the abdomen by a tear gas canister. I think I did not learn of this until I came out of hospital. I spoke to one of the doctors at the French Hospital, where the man was being treated, and was told that his wound, although not life-threatening, was fairly serious. That anyone should have been wounded in this way was, I suppose, due to the inexperience of the British Police in crowd control, and the use of tear gas. I presume the man made a full recovery, as I never heard anything to the contrary.

During the afternoon of 29 November, when I was already in hospital, a contingent of Moderates marched up the British Paddock to the Residency Offices, clamouring for the departure of Dumper and Osborne from the New Hebrides. Prominent among them were the Mayor of Port Vila, Remy Delaveuve, and rather surprisingly, George Kalsakau, who had been, until only a short time previously, the senior Melanesian officer in the British Police. Mr. Champion agreed to receive a delegation from this crowd. Apart from Delaveuve, I do not remember which of the Moderate leaders saw the Resident Commissioner. John Champion did not accept the demand that Dumper and Osborne should go, but promised that a commission would be set up to enquire into what had taken place in the morning. What subsequently occurred to prevent this promise being honoured has been described by Champion himself in his contribution to the book, *Tufala Gavman*, published by the University of the South Pacific in 2002.[41] His position had been made intolerable by the combination of four factors: the intransigence of the VP, the irresponsibility of the Moderates, the lack of co-operation from the FR and last, but not least, the apparent error of judgement which led to the discharge of tear gas against the Moderate protestors.

Either on the day after, or on 1 December, the French High Commissioner in Noumea, M. Eriau, despatched a detachment of *Gardes Mobiles* to Port Vila, apparently to prevent any outbreak of disorder resulting from the incidents of 29 November. Eriau then put pressure on Mr. Champion to send Tim Osborne and Mike Dumper out of the Condominium, saying that failure to take this step might lead to attacks (by French people or francophones) on British persons or property, which he might not be able to prevent. This was a kind of blackmail, and quite outrageous. In the face of it, the BRC had no realistic option, other than compliance with Eriau's demand. Accordingly, four or five days after 29 November, Dumper and Osborne left Port Vila on what was officially described as, special leave. There were, in fact, no attacks on British persons or property, but the two officers concerned could have faced unpleasantness or worse, if they had remained in Port Vila, carrying out their normal duties.

As for myself, unhappily obliged to remain in a hospital bed, when I would have liked to have been supporting Champion during those difficult days, I heard it was being put about in French circles that my illness was of a diplomatic nature. I certainly received no solicitous enquiries as to my health, or hospital visits from any of my French colleagues.

In the event, the Commission of Enquiry promised by Champion on 29 November did not take place, as the French Government made it clear that no French citizen could be summoned to give evidence before it, and the Foreign Office abandoned the proposal. I have no doubt that, if the Commission had sat, and French officials and private citizens been required to testify, the FR would have come out of it very badly. This may have been why the French Government opposed its establishment.

Within a few weeks of 29 November, it was announced that both Gauger and Doyen, respectively the FRC and the Chancelier, were to be replaced. They were succeeded by two graduates, M. Potier and M. Mermet, of the Ecole Nationale d'Aministration, one of the prestigious *Grandes Ecoles*. I never learnt what, if any experience either of them had had in French Overseas Territories or Departments. By some point in the middle of 1978, both Potier and Mermet had also gone.

---

41 John S. Champion, 'John S. Champion CMB, OBE: British Resident and Commissioner, 1975–78,' in *Tufala Gavman: Reminiscences from the Anglo-French Condominium of the New Hebrides*, ed. Brian J. Bresnihan and Keith Woodward, Suva: University of the South Pacific, 2002, pp. 142–54.

Afterword: And what of education?

I have now reached the end of these memoirs. The Condominium finished ingloriously, amid attempted secession by some of the inhabitants of Espiritu Santo, and violence on Tanna. I must leave it to those who may read what I have written over the past year (2010–11), more than thirty years on, and my detailed description of constitutional development, written just before my departure from Port Vila in 1978 to form their own opinion as to why this was so.[42] However, I shall hazard my own tentative analysis, based on my knowledge of the history and antecedents of the Condominium, and my twenty-five years of working with the system.

Firstly, the Condominium was set up as a *pis aller* arrangement, in order to provide the previously rather anarchic New Hebrides with a form of settled government, by two countries, Great Britain and France, which had been colonial rivals for centuries. The Joint Administration, which is a more accurate name for the arrangement than Condominium, had the inherent weakness of not being a properly unified government. On the contrary, its emphasis (as set out in the Anglo-French Convention of 1906) was on the two powers doing only the essential minimum of administration together, whilst preserving separate national control over their own subjects and citizens. This principle led to the establishment of a dualised administrative system, which left plenty of scope for local rivalry between the representatives of the two signatory powers.

In the early years of the Condominium, the exercise by each power of separate control over its own nationals and *ressortissants* (see note 10) led to the abuses described by the English lawyer, Edward Jacomb (n.d.), in his unpublished papers.[43] Because the Convention provided for each Residency to execute on its own nationals the judgements of the Joint Court, Jacomb found that the FR frequently failed to enforce the Court's judgements on French planters convicted of offences against the clauses of the Convention respecting the recruitment and employment of Melanesian labourers. The pressure exerted by the Presbyterian and Anglican Missions in Australia and Britain for these abuses to be remedied was one of the factors leading to the British Government calling for the revision of the Convention. In the Anglo-French Protocol of 6 August 1914, provision was made, at British insistence, for the judgements of the Joint Court, the Courts of First Instance, and the Native Courts to be executed by the RCs jointly.[44] Unfortunately, the Protocol, which was signed two days after the outbreak of the Great War, was not brought into effect until March 1922.

---

42   Woodward, 'Historical Summary.'
43   Jacomb, 'A Family Portrait.'
44   The Courts of First Instance, with jurisdiction over offences against Joint Regulations, and the Native Courts, which tried crime and civil cases between Melanesians, were introduced by the Protocol.

Figure 10. Eratoka Island, also known as Hat Island, Ghost Island or Devil's Island taken from aboard the *Don Quixote*.

Source: Photograph by Michael Allen, November 1958.

Figure 11. Jean Guiart writing up his diary in Maroo village, Emau Island.

Source: Photograph by Michael Allen, November 1958.

The Condominium has been much criticised and mocked as a ridiculous arrangement. While writing these last lines, however, an interesting thought has struck me. We know that Britain was far from anxious to acquire additional colonial responsibilities by involving itself in the New Hebrides. Indeed, it might well have agreed to French annexation of the group in 1885, when approached to that end by France, but for the strong opposition voiced by the Australian Colonies. Since France, with more settlers, and considerable land interests in these islands by the early twentieth century, would not have accepted a British take-over, and since some form of settled government was needed, the Condominium was the only solution. It is my view that the indigenous people of the New Hebrides had reason to be thankful for the Condominium, if one considers the only likely alternative, French annexation. France annexed New Caledonia in 1853 and for many years used it as a penal colony. The Melanesian inhabitants or *canaques* (the French version of the English term kanaka) were not well treated under French colonial rule, and they rose against it in 1878. The revolt was a serious one, and considerable force had to be employed to suppress it. There was another, but less serious reason, rising in 1917. The well-known French anthropologist, Professor Jean Guiart (Figure 11),[45] has severely criticised the treatment of the *canaques*, pointing out that for many years, and well into the twentieth century, they were subjected to a system of forced labour. Guiart described them as second-class citizens, although their political situation has been much improved over recent decades. There was, nevertheless, a serious outbreak of inter-racial violence in the territory in the mid-1980s with both Europeans and Melanesians being killed.

With the obvious exception of the abuses associated with the recruitment and employment of plantation labourers during the early years of the Condominium, the indigenous people of the New Hebrides fared much better under joint Anglo-French administration (or lack of it) than did formerly their Melanesian cousins under purely French rule in New Caledonia. As Guiart, the author of several books and monographs about both the New Hebrides and New Caledonia, has notably pointed out, under the Condominium, New Hebridean villagers were left largely to their own devices, free to manage their own affairs with minimal interference by the administration, which had only a light presence on the ground.[46] The fact that the Government in Port Vila was represented in each of

---

45   Guiart has published extensively on this topic but see especially J. Guiart, 1968, 'Le cadre social traditionnel et la rébellion de 1878 dans le pays de la Foa, Nouvelle-Calédonie,' *Journal de la Société des Océanistes* 24: 97–119; Guiart, 1970, 'Les événements de 1917 en Nouvelle-Calédonie,' *Journal de la Société des Océanistes* 26: 265–82; Guiart, 1982, 'One of the last colonies: New Caledonia,' *Journal of International Affairs* 36(1): 105–112; Guiart, 1985, 'Les canaques, les caldoches et les autres,' in *Regards sur l'actualité, La crise calédonienne*, Paris: La Documentation française 107: 18–31.

46   See J. Guiart, 1978, 'Les Nouvelles-Hébrides,' in *Ethnologie régionale no. 1 Encyclopédie de la Pléiade*, ed. J. Poirier, Paris: Gallimard; Guiart, 1983 [2012], *La Terre est le Sang des Morts*, Paris: Editions Anthropos; Guiart, 1986, 'La conquête et le déclin: Les plantations, cadre des relations sociales et économiques au Vanuatu, ex Nouvelles-Hébrides,' *Journal de la Société des Océanistes* 42: 7–40.

the four Districts by two District Agents, one British and one French, militated against oppressive administration. Villagers who felt aggrieved by the decisions or actions of one of the District Agents could complain to the other *gavman* or administration and there was some playing of one side against the other by New Hebrideans, although I feel the tendency towards this working the system may have been exaggerated, like much else about the Condominium.

In general, it can be said that the rural inhabitants of the Condominium were subject to very little administrative interference. The District Agents held sittings of the Native Court, assisted by two New Hebridean Assessors, when crimes were reported to them. Otherwise offences were dealt with under custom by chiefs and assessors. The downside of what could be regarded as administration by salutary neglect was that, until the post-World War II era, Government did very little for the Melanesian people, leaving it to the various Christian missions to provide, insofar as their resources permitted, rudimentary health and education facilities. On the other hand, the Condominium was not alone in this, since a similar situation existed, for example, in the British Solomon Islands Protectorate. It was to the credit of the French Government that it set up hospitals, staffed by military doctors and Catholic nuns, on Santo and Malekula, as well as in Port Vila.

From the 1950s onwards, government in the New Hebrides took on a more positive form, as development became the watchword. Both the British and French Governments began spending significant sums on both social and infrastructural development—education, health, roads, airfields and wharves. Local Councils were set up to encourage New Hebrideans to provide their communities with minor services and facilities, helped by Condominium grants. The fact that the Condominium was not a truly unified administration adversely affected the development of Local Councils, however, as most French District Agents showed little enthusiasm for them, and gave scant support to the efforts of their British colleagues to encourage and help the councils.

It was, however, in the sphere of educational development that the dual nature of the Condominium was most apparent, and most unfortunate, to use no stronger term. Needless to say, both the Convention and the Protocol made no reference to the education of the indigenous population. There was, therefore, no reason at all why such a question as to which language, English or French, should be taught, should be mentioned in these treaties. Yet this was the issue which, perhaps more than any other, highlighted the essential flaw in the 1906/14 Anglo-French agreement that the New Hebrides should constitute a region of joint influence. This flaw, which can hardly be over emphasised, meant that the two treaties set the scene for the group to become a region of competition and rivalry between the two powers, because they had failed to create a unified system of administration.

The possibility that the education of Melanesian children might become a field of competition between the signatory powers did not emerge, or did not bother them, until the last thirty years before the end of the Condominium. This was simply because both the British and French Governments, and especially the former, were content to leave education to the missions. They at length realised, at more or less the same time in the late 1950s that mission education could not, for lack of resources, go far enough, and that government had to step in.

For the British, this was basically a matter of acting through the network of Presbyterian, Anglican, Church of Christ and village schools which covered the greater part of the New Hebrides, and therefore a majority of Melanesian children. As there was virtually no English-medium secondary education, and no worthwhile teacher training, the British Government would also have to start more or less from the beginning in these fields. My point is that, by taking over English-medium education from the Missions, the British Government would automatically ensure that most New Hebridean children would ultimately speak English, and come under British cultural influence, such as it was.

For France, however, it was altogether different. There were, in 1960, French State schools in Port Vila and Luganville, one in Isangel, Tanna and possibly one or two on Malekula. Apart from these institutions, the teaching of French was in the hands of the Catholic schools, and perhaps a few French Protestant Mission ones on Santo and Malekula. Thus, if France simply copied the British Government, and did no more than upgrade mission schools by increasing, or introducing financial support for them, French-educated francophone Melanesians would remain a minority, since the Catholics and French Protestant missions had far fewer adherents than the combined 'British' missions. From the French viewpoint, this was an anomalous and unacceptable situation, since it was inherent in the Convention and Protocol that France had equal rights in the New Hebrides. Beginning with the Delauney period in the early 1960s and accelerating under Mouradian, Langlois and Gauger, into the mid-1970s, France began a well-resourced programme of improving and extending education in French, especially through the creation of French State schools throughout the Condominium. As it developed, French education policy aimed at getting half of the children into French-medium schools, either Catholic or state run. This was a logical objective from France's point of view, and one of which criticism on my part would be presumptuous. The implementation of the policy, however, inevitably brought about attempts by French District Agents to induce villagers to accept French schools in places where there already existed Presbyterian or other denominational schools.

Proposals to install a French school, where there was a Presbyterian one did not necessarily cause trouble, because French schools charged no fees, and parents with large families found it convenient to reduce the cost of educating their children by putting one or more of them into the French system. Alternatively, as I have indicated earlier, over-vigorous attempts by French District Agents or education officers to obtain agreement for a French school could cause resentment and local disputes.

The problem of potential competition over education was inherent in the administrative and legal system created by the Convention and was not solved before the end of the Condominium. This was probably because there was no politically feasible solution that would have been consistent with the equal rights accorded to each Signatory Power by the Convention/Protocol. It is now academic to look at possible expedients. None of them, such as teaching all New Hebridean children both French and English, or teaching English in some islands or areas, and French in others, would have been free from serious objection from a political or educational standpoint. So it only remains, given the failure of the Condominium in this domain to ask whether, in the long run, it really mattered, that is, whether the lives of many New Hebrideans had been adversely affected.

I have not the knowledge of what happened in Vanuatu post-independence to answer this question satisfactorily. Perhaps the political polarisation between anglophone and francophone Melanesians in the years immediately preceding independence led to francophones suffering from some degree of discrimination in public service employment between 1980 and 1991, when the VP enjoyed sole power. If so, I have not heard of it. During most, if not all, of the years elapsing since 1992, francophone politicians have shared power with the anglophones, and no one party can govern alone, there now being a good deal of political fragmentation, and a lack of stable government. This factor, together with the continued existence of some degree of island identity consciousness, to say nothing of the multiplicity of religious denominations, seems likely to ensure the survival of democracy in Vanuatu.

Figure 12. Keith Woodward and John Champion, the British Resident Commissioner at Bauerfield Airport, Port Vila, on the day of Keith's departure from the New Hebrides, 1 March, 1978.

Source: Photographer unknown, supplied by Brian Bresnihan.

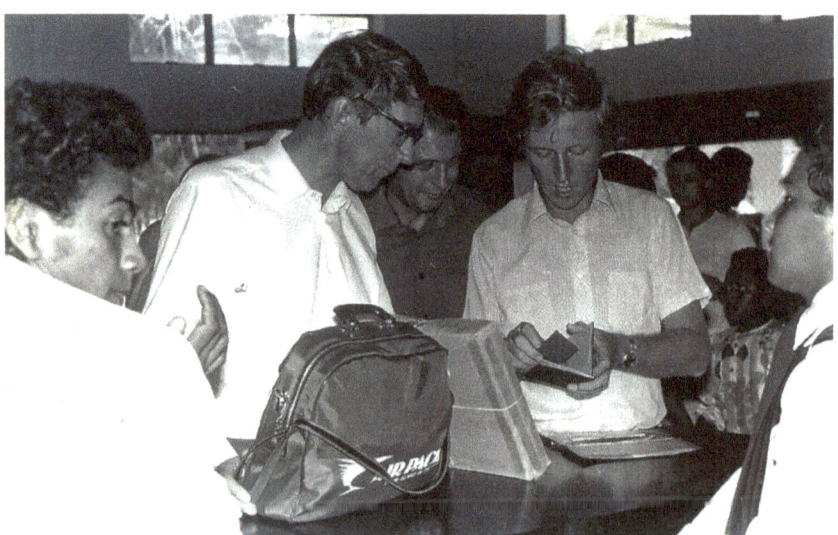

Figure 13. From left: Keith Woodward, Dick Baker and Brian Bresnihan (all colleagues in the British Administration), framed by unidentified New Hebrideans, including an airline official in the bottom right hand corner. Keith was on the point of checking in for his flight on the day of his departure from the New Hebrides. Bauerfield Airport, 1 March, 1978.

Source: Photographer unknown, supplied by Brian Bresnihan.

Concluding thoughts

For family reasons, and because of my deteriorating sight, I sadly left the New Hebrides on 1 March 1978, after just less than twenty-five years in the Condominium (Figures 12 and 13). In later years, I have much regretted my decision to do this, wondering whether I could have made any useful contribution to the process which finally led to Independence. I have tried to console myself with the thought that the electoral system which I originated in 1975 is still in use, although it was not designed with the multiplicity of political parties now existing in Vanuatu in mind, and is therefore less effective.[47] Perhaps the instability of governments which has bedevilled Vanuatu politics since the 1991 split in the Vanu'aku Pati would not have come about had a different electoral system been in place. There is a danger of former Condominium administrators like myself being patronising about Vanuatu politics today and so I shall indulge myself no further on this subject. After weathering a few minor storms since 1980, Vanuatu is still a democracy and I am glad to have played a small part many years ago in its evolution towards self-determination.

---

47 See Howard Van Trease (ed.), 1995, *Melanesian Politics:* Stael Blong *Vanuatu*, Christchurch: Macmillan Brown Centre for Pacific Studies, University of Canterbury and Suva: Institute of Pacific Studies, University of South Pacific.

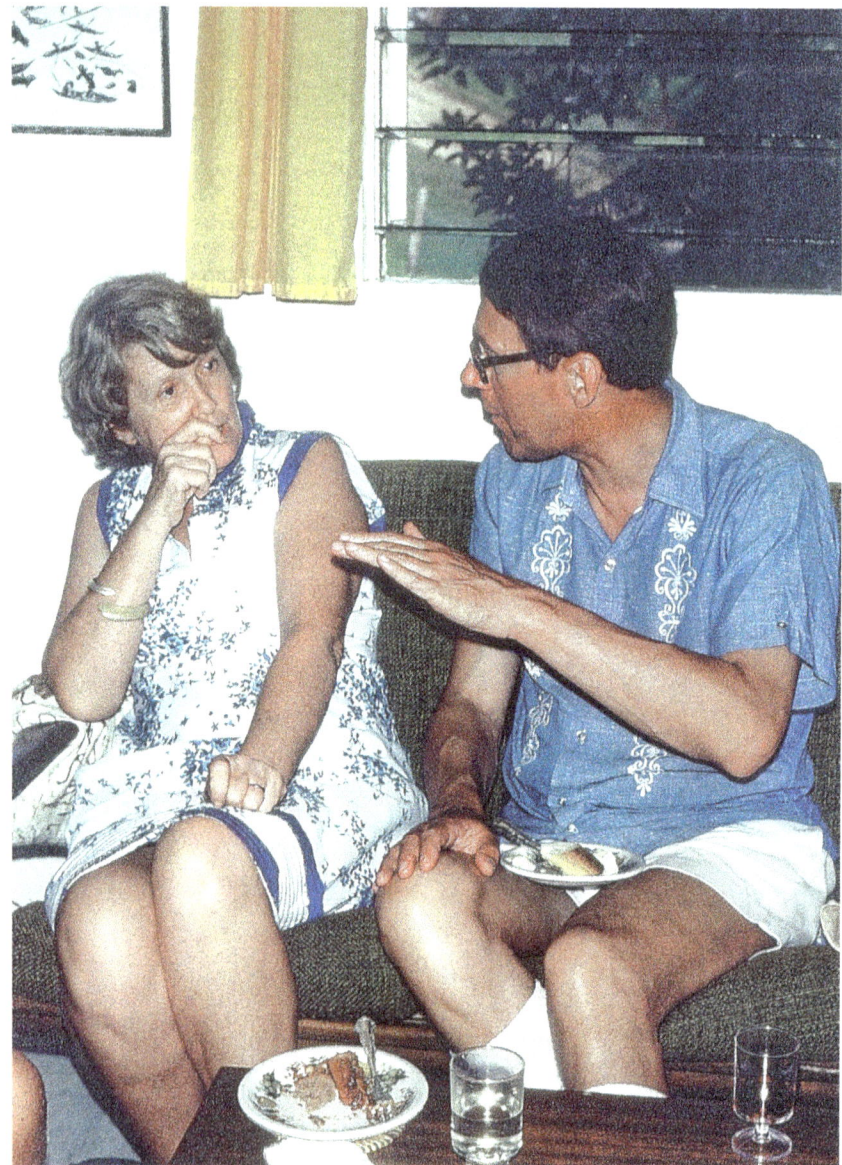

Figure 14. Keith enjoying himself at a lunch party in Port Vila in March 1980, when he paid a return visit to the New Hebrides. He is talking to Olla Reeve, the woman who painted the watercolour of the British Office (Figure 15).

Source: Photograph by Brian Bresnihan.

Figure 15. British Administration Building, water colour, Olla Reeve, ca. 1977, in the collection of Brian Bresnihan.

Source: Photograph by Brian Bresnihan.

References

Beasant, J. 1984. *The Santo Rebellion: an Imperial Reckoning*. Honolulu: Hawaii University Press.

Bernard, P. 1983. *Le Nagriamel: tradition et nationalisme au Vanuatu. Thèse de 3ème cycle*. Paris: Université Paris-X-Nanterre.

Bresnihan, B.J. and K. Woodward (eds) 2002. Tufala Gavman: *Reminiscences from the Anglo-French Condominium of the New Hebrides*. Suva: Institute of Pacific Studies, University of the South Pacific.

Champion, John S. 2002. John S. Champion GMG, OBE: British Resident Commissioner, 1975–1978. In Tufala Gavman: *Reminiscences from the Anglo-French Condominium of the New Hebrides*, ed. B.J. Bresnihan and K. Woodward. Suva: Institute of Pacific Studies, University of the South Pacific, pp. 152–54.

Guiart, J. 1968. Le cadre social traditionnel et la rébellion de 1878 dans le pays de la Foa, Nouvelle-Calédonie. *Journal de la Société des Océanistes* 24: 97–119.

———. 1970. Les événements de 1917 en Nouvelle-Calédonie. *Journal de la Société des Océanistes* 26: 265–82.

———. Les Nouvelles-Hébrides. In *Ethnologie régionale no 1 Encyclopédie de la Pléiade*, ed. J. Poirier, Paris: Gallimard.

———. 1982. One of the last colonies: New Caledonia. *Journal of International Affairs* 36(1): 105–12.

———. 1983 [2012]. *La Terre est le Sang des Morts*. Paris: Editions Anthropos.

———. 1985. Les canaques, les caldoches et les autres. In *Regards sur l'actualité, La crise cal. donienne*. Paris: La Documentation française 107: 18–31.

———. 1986. La conquête et le déclin: Les plantations, cadre des relations sociales et économiques au Vanuatu, ex Nouvelles-Hébrides. *Journal de la Société des Océanistes* 42: 7–40.

Hackford, E. 2002. Edward Hackford: Administrative Officer, 1969–1971. In *Tufala Gavman: Reminiscences from the Anglo-French Condominium of the New Hebrides*, ed. B.J. Bresnihan and K. Woodward. Suva: Institute of Pacific Studies, University of the South Pacific, pp. 276–84.

Hours, B. 1974. *Un mouvement politico-religieux néo-hébridais: le Nagriamel*. Cahiers ORSTOM 11(3–4): 227–42.

———. 1976. Leadership et cargo cult: l'irrésistible ascension de J.T.P.S. Moïse. *Journal de la Société des Océanistes* 32(2): 207–231.

Hutchinson, R.J.S. 2002. Dick Hutchinson: Administrative office 1956–1972. In Tufala Gavman: *Reminiscences from the Anglo-French Condominium of the New Hebrides*, ed. B.J. Bresnihan and K. Woodward. Suva: Institute of Pacific Studies, University of the South Pacific, pp. 301–26.

Jacomb, E. n.d. *Family Portrait*. Micro-MS-Coll-20-2338. University of London, Senate House Library and Alexander Turnbull Library, Wellington, New Zealand.

Kele-Kele, Kalkot Matas 1977. The emergence of political parties. In *New Hebrides: Road to Independence*, ed. Chris Plant. Suva: Institute of Pacific Studies, University of South Pacific, pp. 17–34.

———. 2008. *Nabanga: The Quarterly Newsletter of the British Friends of Vanuatu* 98: 14–15.

Miles, W.F.S. 1998. *Bridging Mental Boundaries in a Postcolonial Microcosm: Identity and Development in Vanuatu*. Honolulu: University of Hawai'i Press.

Parsons, M. 1981. Phoenix: ashes to ashes. *New Internationalist Magazine* 101 (July).

Plant, Chris (ed.) 1977. *New Hebrides: Road to Independence*. Suva: Institute of Pacific Studies, University of South Pacific.

Shears, R. 1980. *The Coconut War: The Crisis on Espiritu Santo*. Sydney and Melbourne: Cassell Australia Limited.

Stevens, J.M. 1995. The Nagriamel movement. In *Melanesian Politics:* Stael Blong *Vanuatu*, ed. Howard Van Trease. Christchurch: Macmillan Brown Centre for Pacific Studies, University of Canterbury and Suva: Institute of Pacific Studies, University of South Pacific, pp. 227–34.

Stuart, A. 2001. *Of Cargoes, Colonies and Kings: Diplomatic Administrative Service from Africa to the Pacific*. London and New York: The Radcliffe Press.

Tabani, M. 2008. The political history of the Nagriamel movement. *Oceania* 78: 332–57.

Van Trease, Howard 1995. Colonial origins of Vanuatu politics. In *Melanesian Politics:* Stael Blong *Vanuatu*, ed. van Trease. Christchurch: Macmillan Brown Centre for Pacific Studies, University of Canterbury and Suva: Institute of Pacific Studies, University of South Pacific, pp. 3–58.

Van Trease, Howard (ed.) 1995. *Melanesian Politics:* Stael Blong *Vanuatu.* Christchurch: Macmillan Brown Centre for Pacific Studies, University of Canterbury and Suva: Institute of Pacific Studies, University of South Pacific.

Woodward, Keith 1978. Keith Woodward – Historical summary of constitutional advance in the New Hebrides, 1954–1977. Canberra: Pacific Manuscripts Bureau, [2001]. Held State Library of New South Wales, Manuscripts, Oral History and Pictures, online: http://acms.sl.nsw.gov.au/item/itemDetailPaged.aspx?itemID=441498, accessed 21 July 2014.

———. 2002. Historical Note. In Tufala Gavman: *Reminiscences from the Anglo-French Condominium of the New Hebrides,* ed. B.J. Bresnihan and K. Woodward. Suva: Institute of Pacific Studies, University of the South Pacific, pp. 16–72.

www.ingramcontent.com/pod-product-compliance
Lightning Source LLC
Chambersburg PA
CBHW060947170426
43197CB00031B/2993